First published in Great Britain by Simon & Schuster UK Ltd, 2010
A CBS Company

Copyright © 2010, Weight Watchers International, Inc.
Simon and Schuster Illustrated Books, Simon & Schuster UK Ltd, First Floor,
222 Gray's Inn Road, London WC1X 8HB

Weight Watchers is a registered trademark of Weight Watchers International, Inc.,
and is used under its control by Weight Watchers (UK) Ltd.

Weight Watchers Publications: Jane Griffiths

Printed in China

ISBN 978-1-84737-610-7

A CIP catalogue for this book is available from the British Library

13 5 7 9 10 8 6 4 2

Pictured on the front cover: Mango and Raspberry Smoothie p26, Lemon Sole Goujons
p145, Potato and Ham Bake p112.
Pictured on the back cover: Thai-style Chilli Chicken on Brown Rice p68, Frozen Fruit Salad
p117, Italian Meatballs p103.

ⓥ This symbol denotes a vegetarian recipe and assumes that, where relevant, free range
eggs, vegetarian cheese, vegetarian virtually fat free fromage frais, vegetarian low fat crème
fraîche and vegetarian low fat yogurts are used. Virtually fat free fromage frais, low fat crème
fraîche and low fat yogurts may contain traces of gelatine so they are not always vegetarian.
Please check the labels.

✿ This symbol denotes a dish that can be frozen.

RECIPE NOTES
Egg size: Medium, unless otherwise stated.
All fruits and vegetables: Medium sized, unless otherwise stated.
Raw eggs: Only the freshest eggs should be used. Pregnant women, the elderly
and children should avoid recipes with eggs that are not fully cooked or raw.
Stock: Stock cubes used in recipes, unless otherwise stated. These should

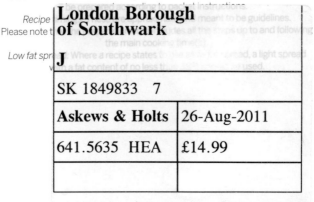

WeightWatchers

HEALTHY FOOD
for hungry families

Karen Miller-Kovach

SIMON & SCHUSTER
A CBS COMPANY

contents

introduction

'I am delighted to be introducing a new cookbook to help busy parents plan and prepare healthy meals for the whole family. In Weight Watchers book *Healthy Parent, Healthy Child* we introduced you to the idea of being a food provider – the person in the family who does the shopping, plans the menus and has a consistent positive attitude to food. Well, this new cookbook is full of inspirational recipes that will help you to make meals into family times that everyone looks forward to – regardless of whether they need to lose a few pounds or not.

Healthy Parent, Healthy Child is not a structured diet programme; it's all about making small consistent changes that lead to everyone in the family eating nutritious food. This cookbook builds on the idea, showing you how to create delicious meals that are full of flavour and made with healthy ingredients.

Newspapers, magazines and TV programmes are constantly warning us that we are storing up trouble for ourselves and for our children if we don't sort out our eating habits now, but it's hard to keep to a nutritious eating plan when there are so many temptations around us. This collection of recipes includes the kinds of foods we all like to eat today, and they are just as attractive and tasty but without the salt and the high levels of fat and sugar in many ready-made meals and takeaways.

Nutritious food needn't be boring – it is delicious food,

as this cookbook proves. There are recipes that will take you right through the week: from breakfast to lunch, from quick and easy midweek meals to occasions when you might want to push the boat out and celebrate in style. All the recipes take into account the way we like to live now: from takeaway-style Chinese dishes to Friday-night curries, from lazy Sunday casseroles to a picnic in the park, from a teenage Mexican fiesta to breakfast smoothies, and imaginative ideas for packed lunch boxes. Every recipe is low in salt, sugar and fat, yet we are certain you won't be able to tell the difference.

Being a food provider means giving your family the chance to try new foods and new cuisines, such as Thai-inspired dishes and Mexican meals. This helps your family to expand their healthy food options at home and when they are out and about, helping them to make the right choice every time. What's more, these recipes are all suitable for real families with a range of children aged from 2–18 years. You will see positive comments and ideas from real life families throughout the book.

Living in a healthy-weight home is all about doing things together as a family. The rules are the same for everyone, no matter whether they are the right weight, slightly overweight or even a little underweight – every one eats the same meals. And doing things together extends right across the board, from shopping for ingredients, to cooking the food and sitting down together as a family to eat. Preteens and teenagers are often keen to try new foods and appear sophisticated – so it's an ideal time to capitalise on this. One of the best ways to make young people aware of what they

are eating, and making healthy food choices, is to get them involved in food preparation and cooking. That's why we have included a whole section of recipes for teenage cooks.

If this message hits home with you, then do refer to the companion book to this collection. *Healthy Parent, Healthy Child* shows how any family can adopt the basics of a healthy lifestyle to create a healthy-weight home; a home where every member of the family has a lifestyle that helps them to stay at a weight that is right and healthy for them.

It will help you tackle those familiar situations that every family faces, from taking regular physical activity to cutting down on all that time spent in front of a TV or computer screen.

As a single parent of two boys, I know it isn't easy bringing up children. I took my work home with me and did the best I could to create a healthy-weight home. I am happy to say that my sons are now independent adults who eat well and have an active lifestyle. I hope this book will add to the message in *Healthy Parent, Healthy Child* and help you to be able to say the same.

Karen Miller-Kovach

the wholesome

What are wholesome foods?

Wholegrains like wholemeal bread, whclewheat pasta, brown rice and high fibre cereals provide B vitamins, phytochemicals (beneficial plant compounds) – and fibre, which boosts feelings of fullness and helps the bowel function normally.

Fruit and vegetables provide a combination of vitamins and phytochemicals that no other type of food can match. They're filling because of their fibre and water content even though most don't have a lot of calories.

Proteins such as lean cuts of beef, lamb, pork and veal, along with skinless poultry, fish, eggs and meatless proteins – pulses, soy products and nuts – are necessary for general health and also make meals more satisfying. Many proteins are important sources of key vitamins and minerals.

Water, calorie-free drinks, low fat and fat-free milk are healthy choices and good alternatives to soft drinks and juices. Milk has the calcium and vitamin D that children's bones use to grow. Water and calorie-free drinks quench thirst without adding extra calories.

Healthy oils such as sunflower and olive oil, in small amounts, supply vitamin E.

Meat

Choose lean meat; trim any fat and throw away any fat that results from cooking.

Bacon, lean back
Beef
Gammon
Ham
Lamb
Mince – of any meat with 7% fat or less
Offal
Pork
Rabbit
Venison
NOT INCLUDED:
Sausages, frankfurters, streaky bacon, burgers, processed meat and fatty meats e.g. luncheon meat, salami, pepperoni, corned beef.

Poultry

Choose lean poultry, remove the skin and throw away any fat that results from cooking.

Chicken
Turkey – including minced turkey

NOT INCLUDED:
Breaded and battered poultry products.

Fish & Shellfish

Any plain fish either fresh or frozen.
Tinned fish should be in water, brine or tomato sauce, not in oil.
NOT INCLUDED:
Breaded and battered fish.

Vegetarian foods

Quorn mince, chunks, deli rashers, plain fillets
Tofu
NOT INCLUDED: Quorn burgers and sausages and other vegetarian burgers and sausages.

Eggs

Eggs, any type

Dairy

Cottage cheese, any type
Fromage frais, low fat
Low fat soft cheese
Quark
Soya milk

Yogurt, low fat or very low fat – any flavour
Skimmed milk – for those over 5 years old Children up to the age of 2 years old should have whole milk. Children between the ages of 2-5 years old can have semi-skimmed milk – please refer to your health visitor for extra advice on this.
NOT INCLUDED:
Processed cheese spreads, full-fat soft cheeses and hard cheeses.

Fruit

Any fruit either fresh or frozen with no added sugar. Tinned fruit must be in water or juice and not syrup.
NOT INCLUDED: Fruit juices and dried fruit.

Vegetables

Any vegetables either fresh or frozen
Tinned vegetables must be in brine and have no added sugar.

foods list

NOT INCLUDED: Frozen or tinned vegetables in sauces or with added flavourings.

Soups
Dried

Homemade with any Wholesome Food List ingredients

Restaurant made

Tinned

NOT INCLUDED: Creamy soups

Beans and pulses
Aduki

Baked (in tomato sauce)

Black eyed

Broad

Butter

Cannellini

Chick peas

Flageolet

Haricot

Kidney

Lentils, red, green or brown

Mixed pulses

Mung

Pinto

Soya

Yellow split peas

Bread
Wholegrain bread and rolls – any type

Reduced-calorie bread and rolls – any type

Breakfast cereals
Cereals must be eaten with skimmed milk (or milk appropriate for the age group) – not as dried cereal.

All-Bran

Bran Flakes

Corn Flakes

Porridge

Puffed Wheat

Rice Krispies

Shredded Wheat

Shreddies

Special K

Weetabix

Grains
Buckwheat

Bulgar wheat

Couscous

Crispbread, wholewheat

Millet

Noodles

Pearl barley

Polenta

Popcorn (air popped, fat free)

Quinoa

Rice – brown or wild

Rice noodles

Semolina

Wholewheat pasta

Drinks
Coffee

Diet drinks – any under 1 calorie per 100 ml

Soda water

Tea

Water or mineral water

NOT INCLUDED: Fruit juices and alcoholic drinks.

Oils
Olive

Rapeseed

Safflower

Sunflower

All above in small amounts e.g. 1-2 tsps.

Low fat cooking spray

NOT INCLUDED: Margarine, butter and other spreads.

.

Condiments, sauces and dressings
Apple sauce (unsweetened)

Artificial sweetener

Baking powder

Beef extract

Bicarbonate of soda

Capers

Cream of tartar

Curry powder

Fat- or oil-free dressings

Gelatine

Gravy granules

Herbs – fresh or dried

Lemon juice

Marmite

Mint sauce

Mustard

Passata

Pepper

Salsa

Soy sauce

Spices – fresh or dried

Stock cubes – any type

Sugar-free jelly

Tabasco pepper sauce

Teriyaki sauce

Thai fish sauce

Tomato purée

Vanilla essence

Vinegar

Wasabi paste

Worcestershire sauce

Yeast extract

start the day

It has been shown that children who eat breakfast tend to have fewer weight problems than those who skip it. Eating breakfast is also linked to maintaining a healthy weight in adults. So make breakfast a regular meal for the whole family, creating a healthy habit that will benefit your children throughout life.

Everyone knows that mornings can be rushed, especially during term time, but smoothies are fun and quick to whizz up, and teenagers can be encouraged to make their own. If you have a little more time, maybe at the weekend or during holidays, try a healthy, low fat, low salt, cooked breakfast for a change.

BREAKFAST BRUSCHETTA

*Turn this into brunch by serving
it with an assortment of other
breakfast items, such as fresh fruit
and low fat yogurt.*

Serves 6 ■ Takes 10 minutes to prepare,
15 minutes to cook ■ Ⓥ

**3 eggs
6 egg whites
low fat cooking spray
1 onion, chopped
1 large tomato, chopped
2 teaspoons dried basil
6 slices wholegrain bread, toasted
   and cut diagonally into 4 pieces
freshly ground black pepper**

1 Using a fork, lightly beat together
the eggs and egg whites.
2 Spray a large, non stick frying
pan with a little cooking spray and
sauté the onion over a medium
heat, stirring frequently until it
starts to turn golden, for about
5 minutes. Add a splash of water
if it starts to stick. Add the tomato
and cook for a further minute.
3 Add the eggs and scramble until
cooked, for about 2 minutes.
Add the basil and season with
black pepper.
4 Top the toast with the egg
mixture and serve immediately.

EGGS BAKED IN ROAST HAM WITH SOLDIERS

*Line the muffin tins with roast ham,
break in some eggs then bake for a
cracking treat.*

Serves 4 ■ Takes 5 minutes to prepare,
12 minutes to cook

**low fat cooking spray
8 thin slices lean ham
4 eggs
freshly ground black pepper
4 slices low calorie bread,
   to serve**

1 Preheat the oven to Gas Mark
6/200°C/fan oven 180°C.
2 Spray four ramekins or individual
ovenproof dishes with the cooking
spray. Line each of these with
two slices of ham, so that there are
no gaps.
3 Carefully crack an egg into each
dish and season with pepper.
Transfer to the oven and bake for
8–12 minutes, depending on how
well you like your eggs cooked.
4 Serve with the bread or toast, cut
into soldiers.

Ⓥ **Variation** For a vegetarian
version, bake the eggs in
hollowed-out large tomatoes.

Adults too

Everyone should eat
breakfast. Children learn
from their parents, so
if your children see you
eating a wholesome meal
at the start of the day
they are more likely to eat
breakfast themselves.

THE ULTIMATE HASH BROWNS

Serves 4 ■ Takes 30 minutes

low fat cooking spray
3 rashers lean back bacon,
  chopped roughly
275 g (9½ oz) cooked green
  vegetables, such as leeks
  and broccoli, chopped roughly
400 g (14 oz) potatoes, peeled,
  cooked and mashed
1 teaspoon Dijon mustard
1 teaspoon wholegrain mustard
1 tablespoon white wine vinegar
4 eggs
freshly ground black pepper

1 Heat a non stick frying pan and
spray with the cooking spray.
Gently cook the bacon for
5 minutes until crispy. Remove
and drain on kitchen paper.
2 Put the green vegetables into
a large bowl. Add the mashed
potatoes, two mustards and
cooked bacon. Season with black
pepper and mix together.

3 Using wet hands, divide the
mixture into four and then shape
each quarter into a large patty or
burger shape.
4 Heat the frying pan you cooked
the bacon in and spray again
with the cooking spray. Gently fry
the potato cakes for 10 minutes,
turning once (do not attempt to
turn until after 5 minutes). Once
cooked, transfer to a plate and
keep warm.
5 Meanwhile, bring a pan of water
to the boil and add the vinegar.
Crack the eggs into a cup and
gently add to the pan. Poach for
5 minutes until opaque. Remove
with a slotted spoon and place on
top of the hash browns. Season
with pepper and serve.

Ⓥ **Variation** For a vegetarian
version, replace the bacon rashers
with three Quorn Deli Bacon Style
Rashers and cook according to the
packet instructions.

BACON, LEEK AND POTATO OMELETTE

This omelette is so tasty – enjoy it for breakfast, brunch or a light meal. Its just the thing for making the most of leftover cooked potatoes.

Serves 2 ■ Takes 15 minutes

low fat cooking spray
2 rashers lean back bacon, chopped
1 leek, sliced
250 g (9 oz) potatoes, peeled, cooked and chopped
4 eggs
2 tablespoons skimmed milk
freshly ground black pepper

1 Spray a non stick frying pan with the cooking spray. Add the bacon and cook over a medium heat for 1–2 minutes. Then add the leek and potatoes and cook gently until the leek is tender and the potatoes are lightly browned, for about 5 minutes. Remove from the frying pan and set aside.

2 In a bowl, beat the eggs and milk together. Pour into the frying pan and cook over a medium heat. As the omelette cooks, bring the set egg towards the centre of the pan with a wooden spatula, so that the raw egg flows over the surface to cook. When almost set, scatter the potato and leek mixture over the surface.

3 Season with black pepper. Cook for another minute or so, then cut in half and serve.

more breakfast ideas

'Research has shown that children who eat breakfast have fewer weight problems than those who skip breakfast – but try telling that to a 15-year-old teen princess. Luckily I discovered that my daughter much prefers to start the day with a savoury dish rather than cereal or toast. Now that she's tried The Ultimate Hash Browns (page 18) and mastered how to make the Bacon, Leek and Potato Omelette (page 20), breakfast arguments are a thing of the past. And I don't have to run out of the door after her, thrusting a banana into her school blazer pocket.

For days when she doesn't fancy a cooked breakfast or there just isn't time to cook, she likes to whizz up a smoothie in minutes – a great way to ensure she is getting at least one or two of her five-a-day fruit and veg. At the weekend when all the family are home and there's no pressure to be up and out of the door, I like to bake a batch of muffins for a late lazy Saturday breakfast. They're very popular after sleepovers too and unsuspecting teenage guests have no idea what a healthy breakfast they're having.

Sharon Amos, mum to Rebecca and Sam

Fruit fun

The Department of Health recommends we eat at least five portions of fruit and vegetables a day as part of a healthy lifestyle. One portion of fruit is equivalent to one apple, a handful of grapes or half a grapefruit.

THREE FRUIT SMOOTHIES

Smoothies are a great way to fill you up with fabulous fresh fruit.

Serves 6 ■ Takes 10 minutes ■ Ⓥ

POMEGRANATE, ORANGE AND MELON

1 pomegranate
2 oranges, mandarins or clementines, peeled and segmented
½ galia melon, peeled, de-seeded and cut into chunks
80 g (3 oz) very low fat natural yogurt
300 ml (½ pint) skimmed milk

1 Scoop the seeds from the pomegranate into a blender, food processor or smoothie maker. Add all the remaining ingredients, then blend until smooth. Sieve to remove the pomegranate pips. Serve chilled.

MANGO, GINGER AND BANANA

200 g (7 oz) mango, without stone, peeled and sliced
1 banana, chopped
1 teaspoon grated fresh ginger
4 tablespoons very low fat natural yogurt
300 ml (½ pint) skimmed milk

1 Blend all the ingredients in a blender, food processor or smoothie maker. Serve chilled.

VANILLA

1 banana
1 teaspoon vanilla essence
300 ml (½ pint) skimmed milk
80 g (3 oz) very low fat natural yogurt

1 Place all the ingredients in a blender, food processor or smoothie maker and blend until smooth. Serve chilled.

Tip Try substituting soya milk and soya yogurt if you are intolerant to dairy products.

GINGER AND MELON COMPOTE

Spice up summer's bounty of melons with our delightful ginger-flavoured sauce.

Serves 6 ■ Takes 15 minutes to prepare, 15 minutes to cook + 30 minutes chilling ■ ⓨ

150 g (5½ oz) artificial sweetener
2 teaspoons ground ginger
1 teaspoon ground cloves,
1 teaspoon ground allspice
440 g (1 lb) watermelon, de-seeded
**   and cut into chunks**
¼ cantaloupe melon, cubed
145 g (5½ oz) blueberries

1 In a small saucepan, combine 60 ml (3 fl oz) of water, the sweetener, ginger, cloves and allspice. Bring to a boil. Reduce the heat and simmer until the sweetener is dissolved, stirring occasionally, for about 15 minutes. Remove from the heat and transfer to a bowl, cover and chill for at least 30 minutes.
2 Divide the watermelon, cantaloupe melon and blueberries evenly between six dishes. Spoon about 1 tablespoon of sauce over each and serve.

Tip The sauce can be prepared a day ahead and stored in the refrigerator.

MANGO AND RASPBERRY SMOOTHIE

If you're struggling to find ways to eat all of your 5-a-day fruit and vegetable portions, a home-made smoothie is an easy way to boost your intake, and it tastes fabulous too.

Serves 2 ■ Takes 5 minutes ■ ⓨ

4 large ice cubes
150 ml (5 fl oz) skimmed milk
1 ripe mango, peeled, stoned and
**   chopped roughly**
1 ripe banana, chopped roughly
100 g (3½ oz) frozen raspberries
juice of a lemon

1 Place all the ingredients except the lemon juice into a liquidiser or blender and blend until smooth. Add lemon juice to taste.
2 Divide between two tall glasses, add drinking straws and serve immediately.

RASPBERRY AND BANANA MUFFINS

Makes 6 ■ Takes 10 minutes to prepare + 30 minutes cooling, 30 minutes to bake ■ Ⓨ ■ ❄

250 ml (9 fl oz) skimmed milk
150 g (5½ oz) semolina
1 small banana, mashed
3 eggs
zest of a lemon
3 tablespoons granulated artificial sweetener
½ teaspoon bicarbonate of soda
100 g (3½ oz) fresh raspberries

1 Preheat the oven to Gas Mark 4/180°C/fan oven 160°C and line a six hole muffin tin with muffin cases. Heat the milk and semolina in a saucepan, stirring until really thick. Leave to cool completely (about 30 minutes) and then cut into small pieces.

2 Whizz the banana and cooked semolina pieces in a food processor until smooth. Add the eggs, lemon zest, sweetener and bicarbonate of soda. Whizz again until smooth.

3 Empty the mixture into a bowl and fold through half of the raspberries. Divide the mixture between the muffin cases and top with the remaining raspberries. Bake in the oven for 25–30 minutes until golden and risen.

Fun and fast breakfast ideas

Smoothies can be made with any combination of fruit. Use the recipes in this chapter to give you ideas and then see what is in season. Older children will love mixing their own recipes too, so get them involved whenever you can.

Experiment with some of the following:

- strawberries
- raspberries
- bananas
- melon
- blackberries
- pineapple
- apples
- mango
- blueberries
- peaches

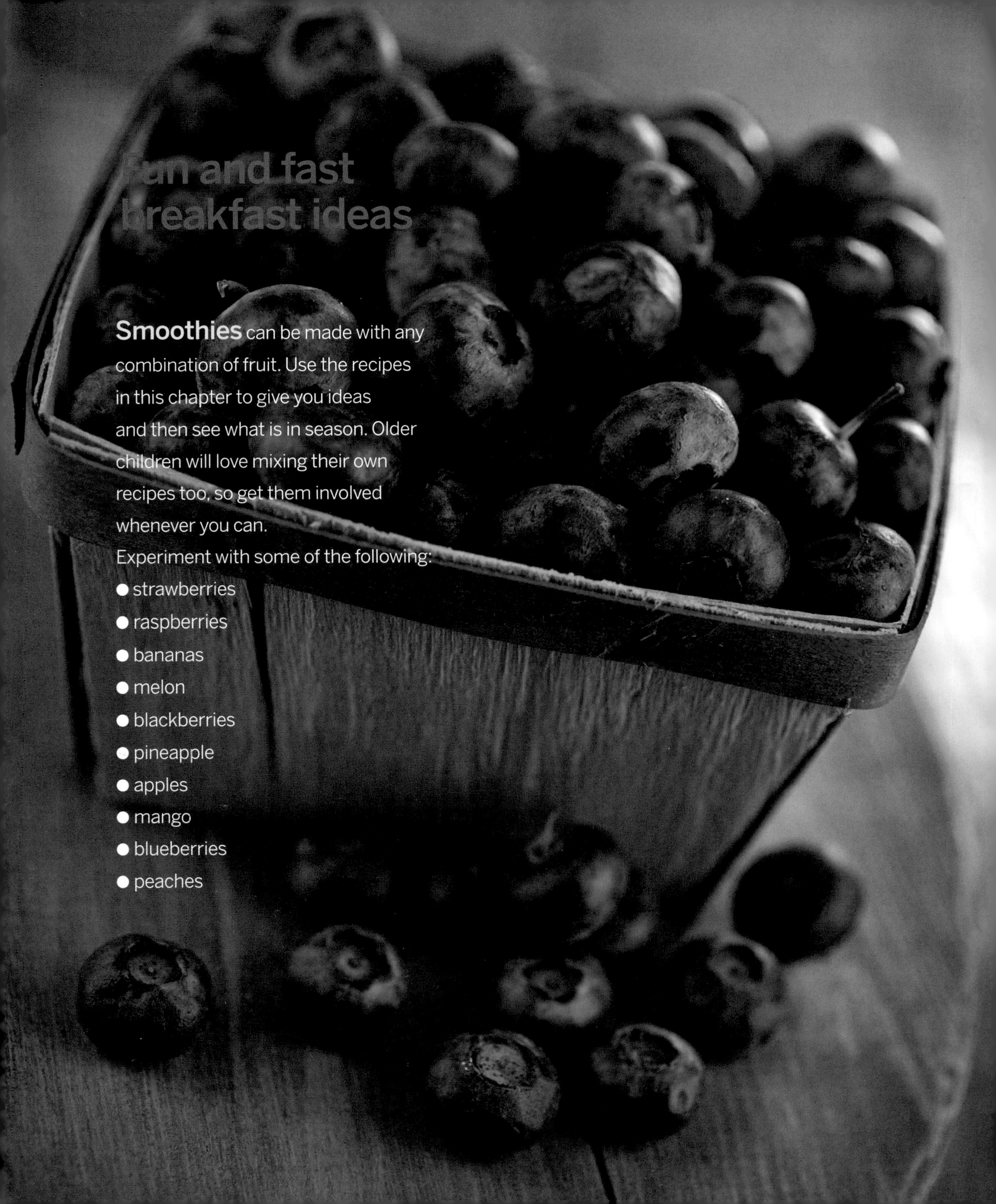

Wholemeal toast is great, but add one of the following for an even more nutritious breakfast:

- grilled mushrooms
- scrambled eggs
- poached eggs
- grilled tomatoes

Fresh fruit makes a great snack but add it to one of the following and it makes a great breakfast too:

- cereal
- muesli
- porridge
- bulgar wheat
- low fat yogurt
- brown rice pudding

lunch on the go

Lunch doesn't have to be the same old sandwiches day after day. Plan ahead and your whole family will have healthy meals full of wholesome foods.

It is up to you to make sure school-age children have a healthy lunch. If they have school lunches, encourage them to make healthy choices; if you provide a packed lunch try stuffing wholemeal pittas with healthy fillings, add crunchy vegetables and make sure you include a portion of fruit. Older children and adults might prefer a flask of soup or a couscous or pasta salad –far more exciting than crisps and high fat foods from a shop.

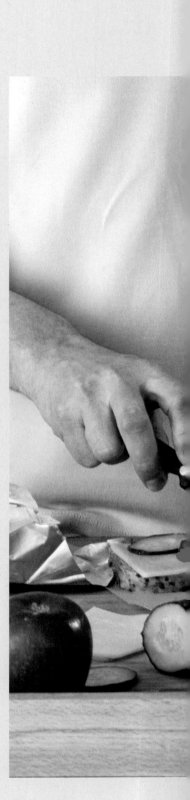

Dinner lady
Take an interest in
the type of food your
children's school provides
at lunchtime. If you feel
there should be healthier
options available, think
about getting together
with other parents to try to
offer suggestions.

ROASTED VEGETABLE COUSCOUS LUNCHBOX

Roasting vegetables in the oven really concentrates the flavour and brings out their natural sweetness. Mixed with couscous, they make for a filling and flavoursome lunch solution.

Serves 2 ■ Takes 35 minutes ■ Ⓥ

1 courgette, trimmed and cut into chunks
1 red pepper, de-seeded and chopped roughly
1 yellow pepper, de-seeded and chopped roughly
1 small red onion, peeled and cut into 6 wedges
200 g (7 oz) butternut squash, peeled, de-seeded and diced
low fat cooking spray
175 g (6 oz) cherry tomatoes
175 ml (6 fl oz) hot vegetable stock
100 g (3½ oz) dried couscous
1 tablespoon chopped fresh basil
25 g (1 oz) wild rocket

1 Preheat the oven to Gas Mark 6/200°C/fan oven 180°C. Toss the courgette, peppers, red onion and squash together in a large roasting tray. Lightly coat the vegetables with the cooking spray and roast in the oven for 15 minutes, stirring half way through.

2 Spray the cherry tomatoes with the cooking spray and add them to the tray of vegetables. Roast for a further 5 minutes, or until the vegetables are tender and beginning to caramelize around the edges.

3 Meanwhile, in a bowl, pour the hot stock over the couscous, stir once and then cover and leave to stand for 5 minutes until the couscous has absorbed the liquid. Fluff up the couscous and stir in the basil. Divide the couscous between two lunchboxes, top with the roasted vegetables and leave to cool.

4 Add the wild rocket once the couscous and vegetables are cool. Seal and chill until ready to eat.

SPICY LENTIL PATTIES

Store cupboard items make up most of the ingredients in these tasty Indian-inspired patties.

Serves 4 ■ Takes 15 minutes to prepare, 25 minutes to cook ■ Ⓥ

low fat cooking spray
4 spring onions, chopped finely
2 garlic cloves, crushed
1 teaspoon fresh root ginger, grated
1 red chilli, de-seeded and chopped finely
2 tablespoons chopped fresh coriander
1 teaspoon ground cumin
400 g can chick peas, drained and rinsed
300 g (10½ oz) green lentils, cooked
freshly ground black pepper
100 g (3½ oz) rocket, to serve

For the mint and coriander relish
25 g (1 oz) fresh mint leaves, chopped roughly
15 g (½ oz) fresh coriander leaves, chopped roughly
1 small onion, chopped finely
a pinch of chilli powder
a pinch of ground cumin
juice of a lemon

1 Preheat the oven to Gas Mark 5/190°C/fan oven 170°C.

2 Mist a non stick frying pan with the cooking spray, then cook the spring onions, garlic, ginger and chilli until softened – about 5 minutes. Mix in the coriander and cumin.

3 Tip the mixture into a blender or food processor and add the chick peas and lentils. Whizz until combined, but not too smooth. Tip into a bowl and season to taste.

4 Using wet hands, shape the mixture into four patties and place on a baking sheet sprayed with a little cooking spray. Bake for 15–20 minutes.

5 Meanwhile, to make the mint and coriander relish, mix together in a food processor, or use a hand held blender. Cover until ready to serve.

6 Serve the patties with the rocket and mint and coriander relish.

WINTER CHICKEN SALAD WITH PASTA

This chicken pasta salad is perfect for a packed lunch – it's healthy, filling and tasty.

Serves 4 ■ Takes 10 minutes to prepare, 15 minutes to cook

250 g (9 oz) wholewheat pasta
1 red onion, sliced thinly
2 celery sticks, chopped
1 green apple, cored and chopped
1 red pepper, de-seeded and chopped
100 g (3½ oz) sweetcorn, thawed
   if frozen
300 g (10½ oz) cooked skinless
boneless chicken, sliced
1 tablespoon chopped fresh parsley
   or chives
150 g (5½ oz) low fat natural yogurt
freshly ground black pepper

1 Bring a pan of water to the boil and cook the pasta according to packet instructions, until tender.
2 Meanwhile, in a large bowl mix together the red onion, celery, apple, pepper, sweetcorn, chicken and parsley or chives. Stir in the pasta and yogurt. Season.
3 Cover and keep chilled for up to 2 days.

Tips For a packed lunch, make sure that you keep the salad in a cool bag with ice packs, or keep refrigerated.

Add 2 teaspoons of medium curry powder to the salad to spice it up.

LUNCHBOX CHICKEN CURRY PASTA

This oh-so-tasty cold chicken pasta will really hit the spot at lunchtime and is perfect for picnics and buffets too.

Serves 4 ■ Takes 15 minutes to prepare, 20 minutes to cook

200 g (7 oz) very low fat natural yogurt
1 tablespoon medium curry powder
low fat cooking spray
250 g (9 oz) skinless boneless chicken breast, cut into bite-sized chunks
300 g (10½ oz) cooked wholewheat pasta, such as spirals or bows
1 red, green or yellow pepper, de-seeded and chopped
¼ cucumber, chopped finely
4 spring onions, sliced finely
freshly ground black pepper

1 Put the yogurt into a bowl and stir in the curry powder.
2 Spray a non stick frying pan with the cooking spray, add the chicken and cook over a medium heat until cooked through. Set aside to cool.
3 Add the pasta, chicken, pepper, cucumber and spring onions to the bowl with the curried yoghurt and stir to combine. Season to taste with black pepper.
4 Pack a portion in your lunch box. Remember to keep it in a cool place, such as an insulated lunch box with an ice pack.

TABBOULEH SALAD

Tabbouleh is a speciality of Lebanon. There are many versions but bulgur wheat, aromatic herbs, tomatoes and spring onions are the basic ingredients. It's traditionally served in Cos lettuce leaves, which act as bowls, but is equally tasty straight from a lunchbox.

Takes 35 minutes + 2 hours chilling ■ Serves 4 ■ ⓨ

200 g (7 oz) bulgar wheat
250 g (9 oz) cherry tomatoes, quartered
20 cm (8 inches) cucumber, peeled, seeds removed and diced
6 spring onions, chopped
4 tablespoons chopped fresh parsley
3 tablespoons chopped fresh mint, plus a sprig to garnish
5 tablespoons lemon juice
1 tablespoon tomato purée
1 garlic clove, crushed (optional)
freshly ground black pepper
4 bowl shaped lettuce leaves such as Cos (Romaine) or Iceberg (optional), to serve

1 Place the bulgar wheat in a large heatproof jug and pour over enough boiling water to cover it. Leave to one side for 30 minutes. Meanwhile, prepare the vegetables and herbs and place all of them, except the garnish and the lettuce leaves, in a large salad or mixing bowl. Mix together the lemon juice, tomato purée, garlic and 2 tablespoons water.
2 Once the wheat is ready, drain it thoroughly (see Tip) and add it to the vegetables. Add the garlic, lemon and tomato mixture and stir well. Season, but bear in mind that the flavour will develop further over the next couple of hours.
3 Cover with clingfilm and leave in the fridge for at least 2 hours. It will keep well if made up to 36 hours in advance. If you are using lettuce leaves in which to serve the tabbouleh, put them in four shallow bowls, check the seasoning and share the tabbouleh between them. Garnish with the reserved mint sprig.

Tip When trying to remove excess moisture from bulgar wheat (or vegetables such as cabbage or spinach), first drain in a fine mesh colander or sieve. Then using a small bowl, push the bowl, bottom side down, onto the bulgur wheat. This will squeeze out any last drops of water.

Pitta power

Get the family involved in food choices. Warm up a pile of pitta breads and set out a range of fillings – grated carrot, chopped cucumber, salad leaves, cherry tomatoes. Children will probably see who can stuff the most in their bread. And with these healthy fillings there's no reason to stop them.

TZATZIKI CHICKEN PITTAS

These Greek-style pittas are a tasty alternative to a kebab. The longer the chicken is marinated before cooking, the more the flavour will develop.

Serves 2 ▪ Takes 30 minutes +
30 minutes marinating

50 g (1¾ oz) low fat natural yogurt
75 g (2¾ oz) 0% fat Greek yogurt
1 tablespoon chopped fresh mint
½ teaspoon dried mint
1 small garlic clove, crushed
2 x 100 g (3½ oz) skinless boneless chicken breasts
4 cm (1½-inch) piece of cucumber, diced
2 wholemeal pitta breads
1 large tomato, sliced

1 Mix the two types of yogurt together with the fresh mint, dried mint and garlic. Set half of the mixture aside to make the tzatziki and pour the other half into a plastic food bag. Cut four shallow slashes in the top of each chicken breast using a sharp knife then place in the bag with the yogurt mixture. Squeeze out the excess air and seal. Place the bag in the fridge and marinate for at least 30 minutes.
2 Mix the diced cucumber into the reserved yogurt mixture and chill the tzatziki until ready to serve.

3 Preheat the grill to medium. Remove the chicken from its marinade and cook under the grill for 7–8 minutes on each side until cooked through. The juices should run clear when the thickest part of the breast is pierced.
4 Place the chicken on a clean chopping board and let it rest for 5 minutes. Warm the pitta breads under the grill for 45–60 seconds on each side.
5 Slice the chicken. Split the pittas open, spoon in some tzatziki and fill with the chicken and tomato slices.

PRIMAVERA PASTA SALAD

A zestful salad, packed full of vital spring vegetables with gutsy flavours and stimulating textures.

Serves 4 ■ Takes 25 minutes ■ ⓨ

250 g (9 oz) wholewheat pasta ribbons
150 g (5½ oz) mange tout
150 g (5½ oz) baby carrots, trimmed
200 g (7 oz) baby sweetcorn
150 g (5½ oz) broccoli, chopped into small florets
4 spring onions, sliced

For the dressing
juice and zest of a lemon
3 tablespoons virtually fat free fromage frais
a small bunch of fresh basil, chopped finely
a small bunch of fresh parsley or chervil, chopped finely
freshly ground black pepper

1 Bring two large saucepans of water to the boil. In one pan cook the pasta for 10–15 minutes, until cooked al dente, and in the other blanch the mange tout, carrots, baby sweetcorn and broccoli for 3–5 minutes, until they are also cooked al dente. Drain the pasta and vegetables and place in a large bowl together.

2 Meanwhile, stir the dressing ingredients together in a small bowl. Add to the pasta and vegetable mixture with the spring onions. Toss together, check the seasoning and serve warm.

Tip This salad can be served warm or cold but it is best warm as the herbs are more aromatic and the vegetables at their most fresh.

LUNCHBOX LAYERED TUNA SALAD

Make a healthy sandwich filling directly in your lunchbox – without the bread.

Serves 1 ■ Takes 10 minutes

1 baby lettuce
1 large tomato, sliced
1 egg, hard boiled
100 g can tuna in brine, drained
¼ small red onion, sliced finely
1 tablespoon capers
1 tablespoon chopped fresh parsley
1 tablespoon vinegar, to season
freshly ground black pepper

1 Place the lettuce leaves directly in the base of a lunchbox. Top with the sliced tomato.
2 Shell the egg and slice it. Place the slices over the tomatoes, then spoon the tuna fish on top.
3 Scatter the red onion, capers and parsley over the top of the tuna, then sprinkle with a few drops of vinegar. Season with black pepper.
4 Seal the lunchbox and keep cool – either in the fridge or in an insulated cool bag with an ice pack.

Variation You can top with skinless roasted chicken, lean ham, lean beef or low fat cottage cheese instead of tuna.

light meals

There are times when you need a light meal that is more than lunch but not a hearty supper – maybe a more substantial lunch before an active afternoon or a quick evening meal between school and after school activities.

These recipes are all quick to make and many can be prepared in advance. Kids in particular will love the turkey patties and chicken drummers.

TUSCAN PUMPKIN AND BEAN SOUP

This soup has a delicious and complex taste.

Serves 6 ■ Takes 15 minutes to prepare, 25 minutes to cook ■ ⓨ

low fat cooking spray
1 onion, chopped
375 g (13 oz) pumpkin, peeled, de-seeded and chopped
850 ml (1½ pints) vegetable stock
400 g can cannellini beans, drained and rinsed
¼ teaspoon dried oregano
freshly ground black pepper

1 Spray a large lidded pan with the cooking spray and set over medium-low heat. Add the onion, cover and cook until tender, stirring occasionally, for about 6 minutes, adding a splash of water if it starts to stick.
2 Stir in the pumpkin, stock, beans and oregano. Simmer for 15–20 minutes.
3 Pour into a blender, or use a hand held blender, and whizz until smooth. You may need to do this in batches. Return to the pan, reheat and season to taste.
4 To serve, ladle into warmed bowls.

TURKEY PATTIES WITH CHILLI APPLE SAUCE

These tasty patties make a delicious light meal. Serve them with a crunchy green salad.

Takes 25 minutes to prepare, 20 minutes to cook + 30 minutes chilling ■ Serves 4 ■ ❄ (patties before cooking)

For the patties
75 g (2¾ oz) fresh wholemeal breadcrumbs (about 2 slices of bread)
3 tablespoons skimmed milk
1 small onion, grated
1 teaspoon dried sage
1 small dessert apple, cored and diced finely
500 g (1 lb 2 oz) lean turkey mince with 7% fat or less
low fat cooking spray

For the sauce
1 red chilli, de-seeded and diced
2 cooking apples, peeled, cored and chopped
1 teaspoon artificial sweetener

1 Combine the breadcrumbs and milk in a mixing bowl, then mix in the onion, sage, diced apple and turkey mince. Using wet hands, carefully shape into 12 patties, cover and chill in the fridge for 30 minutes. Preheat the oven to Gas Mark 5/190°C/fan oven 170°C.
2 Meanwhile, make the sauce. Place the chilli, cooking apples and 2 tablespoons of water in a lidded saucepan. Cover and cook gently for 10 minutes, stirring occasionally, until the apples have softened to a purée. Remove from the heat and stir in the sweetener.
3 Lightly coat a non stick frying pan with the cooking spray. Brown the turkey patties for 1 minute on each side. Transfer to a baking tray lightly coated with the cooking spray and bake for 20 minutes. Serve with the chilli apple sauce.

ADUKI BEAN SALAD

This salad is bursting with fabulous flavours and healthy ingredients – we think you'll love it.

Serves 4 ■ Takes 15 minutes to prepare, 45 minutes to cook and soaking

175 g (6 oz) aduki beans, soaked for
   3–4 hours or overnight
1 vegetable stock cube
finely grated zest and juice of
   a lemon
2 tablespoons white (or red)
   wine vinegar
3 tablespoons tomato purée
1 red onion, sliced finely
225 g (8 oz) canned artichoke hearts,
   drained and halved
225 g (8 oz) roasted red peppers in
   brine, drained and cut into strips
20 baby plum tomatoes, halved
185 g can tuna in brine or water,
   drained
a generous handful of baby spinach
   leaves, lamb's lettuce or mixed
   salad leaves
freshly ground black pepper
1 teaspoon chopped fresh parsley,
   to garnish

1 Rinse and drain the aduki beans and put them in a saucepan. Cover with boiling water. Add the stock cube and stir to dissolve. Simmer for 30-45 minutes, until tender.

2 Meanwhile, mix together the lemon zest, lemon juice, vinegar and tomato purée in a large salad bowl. Add the red onion, artichokes, peppers and tomatoes and stir gently.

3 Drain the cooked aduki beans and rinse under cold running water to cool. Drain again. Add to the salad bowl with the tuna and spinach, lamb's lettuce or mixed leaves. Season with black pepper. Serve, sprinkled with chopped fresh parsley.

Tip Chop four medium tomatoes and use them instead of the baby plum variety, if you prefer.

CAJUN STYLE CHICKEN DRUMMERS

Serves 4 ■ Takes 15 minutes to prepare
+ 1 hour marinating, 45 minutes to cook

2 teaspoons coriander seeds, crushed
1 teaspoon ground cumin
1 teaspoon mild chilli powder
1 teaspoon herbes de Provence
½ teaspoon paprika
1 teaspoon ground allspice
2 teaspoons Dijon mustard
2 tablespoons low fat natural yogurt
8 chicken drumsticks, skin removed
    and trimmed of all fat

For the sweetcorn salsa
198 g can sweetcorn, drained
2 vine tomatoes, de-seeded and
    chopped roughly
1 teaspoon granulated artificial
    sweetener
1 tablespoon white wine vinegar
1 red onion, chopped finely

1 In a bowl, mix together all the spices, mustard and yogurt. Score three shallow cuts into each drumstick and put into a large freezer bag. Add the yogurt and spices and massage into the drumsticks. Leave to marinate for at least 1 hour.

2 Preheat the oven to Gas Mark 5/190°C/fan oven 170°C and line a baking tray with foil. Put the drumsticks on the baking tray and bake in the oven for 40-45 minutes, until cooked and the juices run clear.

3 Meanwhile, mix together all the salsa ingredients and chill until needed. Serve with the drumsticks.

GOOD IDEAS

School run

Be ready when the children come bursting in after school – have a bowl of fruit on the table or carrot and celery sticks in the fridge. And hide the biscuit tin away – or, better still, don't have a biscuit tin.

TURKEY AND MANGO NOODLE SALAD

Serves 4 ■ Takes 25 minutes

125 g (4½ oz) mung bean vermicelli
   (glass noodles)
low fat cooking spray
4 garlic cloves, chopped finely
400 g (14 oz) lean turkey mince
   with 7% fat or less
2.5 cm (1 inch) piece of fresh root
   ginger, chopped finely
1 or 2 small red chillies, de-seeded
   and chopped finely
a bunch of spring onions,
   chopped finely
juice of 2 limes
4 tablespoons soy sauce
100 ml (3½ fl oz) vegetable stock
2 ripe mangoes, peeled, stoned
   and sliced
a small bunch of fresh coriander,
   chopped
a few sprigs of mint, chopped
2 Little Gem lettuces, shredded
4 lime wedges, to serve

1 Place the noodles in a large bowl, cover with boiling water and leave to stand for 5 minutes, or as directed on the packet, then drain. Return to the bowl and roughly chop with scissors.

2 Heat a large, non stick frying pan or wok and spray with the cooking spray. Stir fry the garlic for a few seconds, until golden and then add the turkey mince, breaking up with a wooden spatula. Stir fry for 4 minutes until browned.

3 Add the ginger, chillies, spring onions, lime juice, soy sauce, vegetable stock and noodles. Stir together and heat through for 2 minutes.

4 Remove from the heat and stir through the sliced mango, coriander and mint.

5 Place a pile of lettuce on each serving plate or bowl and spoon on the turkey and noodle mixture. Serve with lime wedges to squeeze over.

CHUNKY BEAN AND TOMATO SOUP

This is a main course soup full of interesting tastes and textures.

Serves 4 ■ Takes 5 minutes to prepare, 25 minutes to cook ■ ⓨ

250 g (9 oz) aduki beans, soaked for 3–4 hours or overnight
low fat cooking spray
1 onion, chopped
2 carrots, chopped
2 celery sticks, chopped
6 large tomatoes, chopped
1.2 litres (2 pints) vegetable stock
1 teaspoon dried oregano
freshly ground black pepper

1 Rinse and drain the aduki beans and put them in a saucepan. Cover with boiling water and simmer for 30–45 minutes, until tender, then drain.
2 Heat a large, lidded saucepan and spray with the cooking spray. Add the onion and stir fry for 5 minutes until softened, adding a little water if necessary to prevent it sticking.
3 Add the carrots, celery and tomatoes and cover. Cook for 15 minutes on a low heat, stirring occasionally.
4 Add the stock, oregano and beans and bring to the boil. Season with black pepper and serve.

WATERCRESS SOUP

This creamy soup is a great choice to fill you up and keep you satisfied.

Serves 4 ■ Takes 30 minutes ■ ⓨ ■ ❀

low fat cooking spray
3 leeks, trimmed, rinsed and sliced
350 g (12 oz) potatoes, peeled and diced
1 litre (1¾ pints) vegetable stock
75 g (2¾ oz) watercress
150 ml (¼ pint) skimmed milk
freshly ground black pepper

1 Heat a large, lidded saucepan and spray with the cooking spray. Stir in the leeks, then add 2 tablespoons of water, cover and cook gently for 5 minutes.
2 Add the potatoes and stock, bring the soup to the boil, cover and simmer for 15 minutes or until the potatoes are tender.
3 Stir the watercress into the pan and add the milk, then liquidise the soup in batches and return to the pan. Gently reheat the soup and season with black pepper before serving.

soup glorious soup

I swear by soup. I make vats of it; it's so quick and easy and a great way of helping us get our five a day. It's also good for using up the odd celery stick or carrot or whatever's lurking in the fridge that might not be crunchy enough to enjoy raw. In fact my children have an affectionate name for my soup – 'bendy' vegetable soup.

The brilliant thing about blending soup is that it disguises what veg you've used when you blitz it up. It was useful for fooling the children when they were younger. No more cries of: 'I hate carrots' or 'Yuk, parsnips.' Adding flavourings helps – one of my favourites is cumin.

I tend to make a pot of soup on Sunday – I get Megan, 12, and Dominic, nine, to do the peeling and chopping. It's ideal when Dominic gets home from school on Mondays, as he has to go straight out again to cubs but he just has time for a bowl of soup before he leaves. Tuscan Pumpkin and Bean Soup (page 46) and Chunky Bean and Tomato Soup (page 52) are both hearty nutritious soups that fit the bill perfectly.
Michelle Ashwell, mum to Megan and Dominic

Spice is nice

Don't be put off by spicy sauces – give them a try. Spicy does not necessarily mean hot and you might find you like the different flavours. If you or your family find them too spicy, reduce the amount of spice you use and try again.

LAMB KEBABS WITH SPICY SAUCE

Although these are ideal hot, they are just as tasty eaten cold with a salad in your lunchbox. Just take the dip separately.

Serves 2 ■ Takes 20 minutes ■ ❄ (kebabs only)

For the kebabs

225 g (8 oz) lean lamb mince with 10% fat or less
1 small onion
1 garlic clove
1 teaspoon coriander seeds, crushed
2 tablespoons fresh coriander
freshly ground black pepper

For the sauce

1 garlic clove, crushed
2 tablespoons Thai fish sauce
2 tablespoons lime juice
1 small red chilli, de-seeded and chopped finely
1 tablespoon white wine vinegar or rice vinegar
1 tablespoon granulated artificial sweetener

1 Soak six bamboo skewers in a bowl of water for at least 10 minutes to prevent them from burning under the grill.
2 Meanwhile, to make the sauce, combine the sauce ingredients in a small screw top jar, add a tablespoon of water and shake well.

3 To make the kebabs, put the kebab ingredients in a food processor, season well and combine until it comes together into a ball. (If you don't have a food processor, crush the garlic clove, and chop the other ingredients as finely as possible. Use wet hands to mix and combine them together.)
4 Divide the mixture into six and use your hands to shape the meat into 'sausages'. Push the bamboo skewers through the middle of the sausage shapes. You can cook them immediately, or chill until required.
5 Preheat the grill to high (or ensure your barbecue is ready). Grill or barbecue for 10 minutes, turning occasionally until browned all over and cooked through. Serve with the dipping sauce and a salad. If reserving for a lunchbox the next day, wrap in clingfilm and refrigerate as soon as they have cooled.

Variations Although the dipping sauce is spicy, the kebabs are not. If you like your food with a real kick, add ½ red chilli or ½ teaspoon chilli flakes to the kebab mixture. You can also substitute the lamb with lean pork or turkey mince.

Tip Use ½ a small red chilli if you don't want the sauce to be too spicy.

WARM LEMON COUSCOUS WITH COD AND MUSHROOMS

A zesty alternative to cod and chips.

Serves 2 ■ Takes 15 minutes

175 g (6 oz) dried couscous
a kettle full of boiling water
finely grated zest and juice from
a lemon
1 small onion, chopped finely
250 g (9 oz) cod fillet, fresh or frozen
175 g (6 oz) button mushrooms,
sliced
175 g (6 oz) green beans, trimmed
4 teaspoons extra virgin olive oil
2 tablespoons chopped fresh flat
leaf parsley,
freshly ground black pepper

1 Put the couscous in a colander or steamer in the sink. Pour some boiling water through the couscous, breaking up the lumpy grains with a fork. Drain. Stir in half the lemon zest. Set aside.
2 Put the onion, cod, mushrooms and green beans in a large saucepan. Add enough hot water just to cover the fish. Set the steamer or colander with the couscous over the saucepan and slowly bring to the boil. Reduce the heat and simmer for 5–6 minutes, or until the fish begins to flake.

3 Meanwhile, mix together the olive oil, remaining lemon zest, lemon juice, half the parsley and black pepper to taste.
4 Lift the steamer or colander off the saucepan. Carefully transfer the fish to a chopping board, remove the skin and flake it gently.
5 Drain the vegetables and stir into the couscous, with half the dressing. Arrange the couscous on two plates, divide the fish evenly between the couscous and drizzle on the remaining dressing.
6 Garnish with the remaining parsley and serve.

SMOKED TROUT AND POTATO SALAD

This salad can be served slightly warm or, once it is cool, packed into a lunchbox to take on a picnic the next day.

Serves 2 ■ Takes 25 minutes

350 g (12 oz) baby new potatoes,
halved
100 g (3½ oz) low fat natural
fromage frais
2 teaspoons coarse grain mustard
1 teaspoon Dijon mustard
6 cornichons (mini gherkins),
diced finely
2 spring onions, sliced thinly
75 g (2¾ oz) baby spinach leaves
125 g (4½ oz) smoked trout fillets

1 Bring a pan of water to the boil and cook the potatoes for 15 minutes or until tender.
2 Meanwhile, mix the fromage frais together with the two mustards, cornichons and spring onions to make the dressing.
3 When the potatoes are ready, drain and leave them to cool for 5 minutes before mixing them with the dressing.
4 Divide the spinach leaves between two bowls and spoon the potatoes on top. Break up the trout fillets into chunky flakes and scatter over the potatoes.

Snack attack

Light meals are not snacks
but meals in themselves.
However, toddlers and
young children need regular
snacks to keep them going
through the day. Snacks
should be wholesome and
nutritious (see p62–63
for ideas).

SPINACH AND ROASTED RED PEPPER FRITTATA

Make this delicious frittata for an easy vegetarian meal.

Serves 6 ■ Takes 10 minutes to prepare,
20 minutes to cook ■ Ⓥ

350 g (12 oz) new potatoes, scrubbed
250 g (9 oz) spinach
low fat cooking spray
200 g (7 oz) roasted red peppers in
**   brine, drained**
4 large eggs
100 g (3½ oz) low fat soft cheese
6 tablespoons skimmed milk
freshly ground black pepper

1 Bring a pan of water to the boil
and cook the potatoes for
15–20 minutes, until tender. Drain
thoroughly. Once cool, slice thinly.
2 Meanwhile, cook the spinach
in a tiny amount of water for
3–4 minutes, until the leaves
wilt. Drain well, squeezing out the
excess moisture with the back of a
spoon. Chop roughly.
3 Preheat the grill to medium high.
4 Heat a large, non stick frying
pan and spray with the cooking
spray. Add the sliced potatoes
and spinach, then tear in the
roasted peppers.
5 Beat the eggs, soft cheese and
milk together. Season with pepper,
then pour into the pan. Cook on the
hob over a low heat until the base
sets, then transfer to the grill to
set and brown the surface. Check
with a knife to make sure that the
frittata has set completely, cooking
for a little longer if needed.

Healthy snacks

Snacks should be wholesome and nutritious and should not be confused with treats, which are high in calories but not nutritious. Here are some suggestions:

A piece of fresh fruit, such as a banana, orange or apple Fresh fruit salad Sticks of raw carrot, celery, cucumber and pepper Mini sandwiches made with wholemeal bread or wholemeal pittas and filled with low fat soft cheese and cucumber Bagels Crumpets Plain popcorn Small pots of low fat yogurt or fromage frais

Super salads

Salads don't have to mean limp lettuce. Try assorted leaves, including mixes that contain rocket or mizuna for a spicy flavour or herbs for a fresh taste.

Add beans and other pulses such as chick peas to salads, as well as sprouting beans for some fresh crunch and flavour.

weekday winners

Regular mealtimes and sitting down together as a family every night will help reinforce the healthy eating message. However, time is often tight during the week and it's easy to fall back on pre-prepared foods.

With just a little preparation you can cook wholesome, quick meals for the whole family. There are real family favourites here and some delicious healthy versions of your favourite takeaways – perfect for a Friday night in with the family.

MUSHROOM AND SWEET ONION PASTA

Serves 4 ■ Takes 25 minutes ■ ⓥ

350 g (12 oz) wholewheat pasta
low fat cooking spray
250 g (9 oz) mushrooms, sliced
4 onions, sliced finely
300 ml (½ pint) vegetable stock
leaves from 4 fresh thyme sprigs or
 2 teaspoons dried thyme
freshly ground black pepper

1 Bring a pan of water to the boil and cook the pasta according to the packet instructions. Drain and keep warm.
2 Meanwhile, spray a large, non stick frying pan with the cooking spray and put on a high heat. Stir fry the mushrooms and onions until they are golden brown. Add the stock and thyme and turn the heat down to a simmer.
3 Simmer until most of the stock has evaporated and the onions are soft – about 15 minutes. Season with pepper and toss together with the pasta. Serve immediately.

HOT BEEF NOODLES

Succulent strips of beef with bright vegetables and noodles and a tasty sauce. It makes a supremely quick meal and needs no accompaniment.

Serves 4 ■ Takes 25 minutes

low fat cooking spray
400 g (14 oz) lean beef steak,
 trimmed of all fat and sliced
 into thin strips
4 shallots or 2 red onions,
 sliced finely
2 garlic cloves, sliced finely
2 red peppers, de-seeded and sliced
1 head of broccoli, sliced into florets
1 teaspoon Tabasco sauce
4 tablespoons Worcestershire sauce
4 tablespoons soy sauce
1.2 litres (2 pints) vegetable stock
200 g (7 oz) thin or medium egg
 noodles
a bunch of coriander, chopped
 (optional)
freshly ground black pepper

1 Spray a large, lidded, non stick frying pan or wok with the cooking spray. Season the beef strips with pepper and stir fry until they are browned all over. Remove to a plate and set aside.
2 Spray the pan again and add the shallots or onions and garlic. Stir fry for 2–4 minutes, adding a little water to stop them sticking, until golden and softened.
3 Add the peppers and broccoli and stir fry for a few minutes until golden on the edges. Then add the beef, Tabasco sauce, Worcestershire sauce, soy sauce, stock and noodles.
4 Cover the pan, bring to the boil and simmer for 5 minutes, until the sauce is reduced a little and the noodles tender. Serve scattered with coriander, if using.

THAI-STYLE CHILLI CHICKEN ON BROWN RICE

Capture the flavours of Thailand in this easy stir fry.

Serves 4 ■ Takes 15 minutes to prepare, 30 minutes to cook + 1 hour marinating

2 garlic cloves, crushed

1 lemon grass stem, chopped very finely

1 tablespoon fresh ginger root, grated

1 red chilli, de-seeded and chopped finely

2 tablespoons fresh coriander, chopped

juice of a lime

1 tablespoon soy sauce

350 g (12 oz) skinless boneless chicken breast, sliced into strips

300 g (10½ oz) dried brown rice

a kettle full of boiling water

low fat cooking spray

4 shallots, sliced thinly

1 carrot, peeled and cut into fine strips

100 g (3½ oz) sugarsnap peas or mange tout, halved

2 heads pak choi, shredded roughly

1 In a bowl, mix together the garlic, lemon grass, ginger, chilli, coriander, lime juice and soy sauce. Add the chicken strips then cover and leave to marinate for about 1 hour.

2 Put the rice into a saucepan. Cover with boiling water and cook for about 30 minutes, or until tender.

3 Ten minutes before the rice is ready, spray a wok or large non stick frying pan with the cooking spray and heat until hot. Stir fry the chicken pieces for 5–6 minutes, then add the shallots, carrot and sugarsnap peas or mange tout. Cook for another 2–3 minutes then add the pak choi and cook until wilted – about 2 more minutes.

4 Drain the rice and serve with the chicken stir fry.

Variation If you wish, use turkey stir fry strips instead of chicken.

COURGETTE ROSTI WITH CHILLI MINT SALSA

Rosti is a grated vegetable, usually potato, which is fried into a crispy pancake. This version with courgette and dill is lovely with the spicy salsa.

Serves 4 ■ Takes 15 minutes to prepare, 10 minutes to cook ■ Ⓥ

300 g (10½ oz) courgettes, trimmed and grated coarsely
300 g (10½ oz) potatoes, scrubbed and grated coarsely
2 tablespoons fresh chopped dill
low fat cooking spray
freshly ground black pepper

For the salsa
16 cherry tomatoes, quartered
½ cucumber, chopped
8 fresh mint leaves, shredded
2 red chilli, de-seeded and diced
1 red onion, sliced thinly
2 tablespoons lemon juice

1 In a large bowl, mix together the grated courgettes and potatoes and squeeze to remove excess liquid. Stir in the dill and season with pepper.
2 Spray a large, non stick frying pan with the cooking spray and heat until sizzling. Place four spoonfuls of the courgette mixture well apart in the pan and flatten with the back of a spatula, pressing down hard to make it as thin as possible.
3 Cook for 4–5 minutes before inverting on to a plate then slipping it back into the pan to cook the other side. Cook for a further 3–4 minutes until golden and crispy.
4 Meanwhile, make the salsa by mixing together all the ingredients and season.
5 Serve each rosti topped with the salsa.

Tip Grate the courgettes and potatoes in a food processor to save time and effort. If you can't get fresh dill, use 2 teaspoons of dried dill.

GOOD IDEAS
Easy marinating
Most marinade times are the suggested minimum. If you are planning to cook a recipe that needs marinating, and you know you will be short of time, mix all the ingredients together in a glass bowl before you leave the house in the morning. Add the meat or fish to the marinade, cover with clingfilm and leave it in the fridge. It will be ready to cook when you get home.

BUBBLE AND SQUEAK

Bubble and squeak makes a great last-minute supper dish. Serve it with dry fried eggs (i.e. eggs fried in a non stick pan with no oil) and a cherry tomato salad enhanced with a finely chopped shallot or red onion and a smattering of balsamic vinegar.

Serves 4 ■ Takes 35 minutes ■ ⓨ

4 large potatoes, about 800 g (1 lb 11 oz), peeled, chopped and cooked, or use leftover boiled potatoes
600 g (1 lb 5 oz) Brussels sprouts or cabbage, chopped and boiled until soft, or use leftover green vegetables
low fat cooking spray
freshly ground black pepper

1 Mash the potatoes and mix in the chopped vegetables with a little pepper. Heat a non stick frying pan and spray with the cooking spray.
2 Tip the potato mixture into the hot pan and squash down with a fish slice until the mixture covers the bottom of the pan and is more or less flat on top.
3 Turn the heat to very low and cook for 10–15 minutes. Using the fish slice, turn over the bubble and squeak, which should now be golden brown on the bottom. Squash it down again and cook for a further 10 minutes until golden on the bottom again. Serve.

Tip It does not matter if you cannot turn the bubble and squeak over in one piece. Just make sure it is cooked throughout before serving.

Start small

Don't try to change everything at once. Start small by switching from oil to a low fat cooking spray or choosing lean turkey mince instead of fatty beef mince. Your family will accept change more easily if it comes in stages.

QUICK TURKEY COTTAGE PIE

This wholesome and satisfying supper dish is great served with peas and carrots. It's wonderful for all the family and makes the perfect cosy evening meal.

Serves 4 ■ Takes 10 minutes to prepare, 20 minutes to cook ■ ❄

500 g (1 lb 2 oz) potatoes, peeled and cubed
4 tablespoons hot skimmed milk
1 tablespoon chopped fresh parsley or ¼ teaspoon ground nutmeg (optional)
500 g packet lean turkey mince with 7% fat or less
low fat cooking spray
2 garlic cloves, crushed
½ teaspoon dried thyme, oregano or mixed herbs
4 spring onions, chopped
500 ml (18 fl oz) chicken stock
1 tablespoon wholemeal breadcrumbs
freshly ground black pepper

1 Bring a pan of water to the boil and cook the potatoes for 10–12 minutes, until just tender. Drain well and then mash them until smooth.

2 Beat in the hot milk, parsley or nutmeg, if using, and season with pepper. Set the mash aside.

3 Meanwhile, heat a large, non stick frying pan and add the mince in small amounts, stirring quickly to break it up. Spray the mince with the cooking spray and cook until it becomes crumbly.

4 Add the garlic, herbs and spring onions. Cook for 2 minutes.

5 Stir in the stock and raise the heat. Simmer for 10 minutes until the mixture has thickened and reduced down. Season with black pepper.

6 Preheat the grill. Spoon the mince mixture into an ovenproof dish. Top with the potatoes, spreading them evenly with a fork. Sprinkle over the breadcrumbs.

7 Place the dish under the grill until the top turns lightly golden. Serve on four warmed plates.

Variation For an even quicker meal, serve the mince on its own with the potatoes, plain boiled, and sprinkled with chopped parsley.

BARBECUED LAMB CHOPS WITH CHARGRILLED VEG

Lean lamb chops taste fabulous cooked on the barbecue.

Serves 4 ■ Takes 10 minutes to prepare, 15 minutes to cook

8 lamb chops, trimmed of all fat
1 garlic clove, crushed
30 g (1 oz) fresh rosemary, chopped, plus an extra sprig for the barbecue (optional)
1 courgette, sliced diagonally
1 red pepper, de-seeded and sliced into 8 pieces
1 yellow pepper, de-seeded and sliced into 8 pieces
175 g (6 oz) asparagus spears
low fat cooking spray
freshly ground black pepper

1 Preheat the barbecue or grill pan. Rub the garlic and rosemary into the lamb chops and season with black pepper.
2 Spray the vegetables with the cooking spray.
3 Barbecue or grill the lamb chops and vegetables for 8–10 minutes, turning often. If you wish, add an extra rosemary sprig to the barbecue or grill pan for extra flavour and aroma.
4 Divide the lamb chops and vegetables between four plates and serve at once.

Tip Use other vegetables if you prefer – such as tomatoes on the vine, aubergine slices and red onion.

GOOD IDEAS

Easy living
Barbecuing is a fun and healthy way to cook. You need very little fat and the food tastes great. If you don't have a barbecue, or it's too cold or rainy, try using the grill or a griddle pan on the hob.

takeaway 'at home'

When I went back to work after maternity leave, I told my husband there were going to be some changes. We'll still have takeaways, but we're going to make our own. Chinese is a takeaway favourite in our household – and it's a surprisingly good choice for kids too, as they love noodles.

My three-year-old Harry is mad about chicken at the moment so he 'helps' me to cook Thai-Style Chilli Chicken on Brown Rice (page 68). He loves One Pot Spicy Chicken and Rice (page 78) too.

I'm even introducing baby Lily to new tastes. Although she's just eight months old, she has tried and enjoyed homemade egg fried rice, for example. By encouraging her to taste many different foods now, I know I'm laying the foundations for her to be a good eater in the years ahead. Any takeaway-style dishes made at home are going to be healthier – and cheaper – so you can't lose.

Rachel Fryer, mum to Harry and Lilly

CHINESE-STYLE RICE AND HAM

Serves 4 ■ Takes 20 minutes to prepare, 25 minutes to cook ■ ❄ (without the egg)

225 g (8 oz) dried brown rice
low fat cooking spray
1 onion, finely chopped
1 teaspoon Chinese 5 spice powder
1 carrot, peeled and grated
75 g (2¾ oz) frozen peas
1 red pepper, de-seeded and diced
75 g (2¾ oz) wafer-thin lean ham, shredded
1 tablespoon soy sauce
2 eggs, beaten

1 Bring a large pan of water to the boil and cook the rice according to the instructions on the packet. Drain and leave to cool and dry out a little.

2 Spray a large, non stick frying pan or wok with the cooking spray, heat and stir fry the onion until softened. Stir in the Chinese 5 spice powder, carrot, peas and red pepper. Stir fry for a further 5 minutes. Add the rice, stir well and heat through. Toss in the ham and soy sauce.

3 Spray a small non stick frying pan with the cooking spray and heat gently. Beat the eggs with 2 tablespoons of cold water and pour into the pan. Cook gently until the egg sets and you have a flat pancake-type omelette. Transfer to a board and slice into thin strips.

4 Pile the rice and vegetables into a serving dish and arrange the egg strips over the top in a lattice pattern.

Variation Add 50 g (1¾ oz) peeled prawns to this recipe.

ONE POT SPICY CHICKEN AND RICE

A simply scrumptious all-in-one rice dish that is a meal in itself.

Serves 4 ■ Takes 20 minutes to prepare, 20 minutes to cook

low fat cooking spray
350 g (12 oz) skinless boneless chicken breasts, diced
1 onion, chopped roughly
1 yellow pepper, de-seeded and chopped roughly
1 courgette, chopped roughly
2 garlic cloves, crushed
1 teaspoon paprika
a pinch of chilli flakes
1 teaspoon dried rosemary
175 g (6 oz) dried brown basmati rice
230 g can chopped tomatoes
350 ml (12 fl oz) boiling water
410 g can kidney beans, rinsed and drained
freshly ground black pepper

1 Lightly coat a lidded casserole dish with the cooking spray and brown the chicken for 4–5 minutes over a high heat. Transfer to a plate. Add the onion, pepper and courgette to the casserole and fry for 3 minutes.

2 Stir in the garlic, spices, rosemary and rice and fry for 1 minute, then return the chicken to the casserole dish. Add the tomatoes and boiling water.

3 Season with black pepper, bring to a simmer, and cover. Reduce the heat to a very low setting and cook for 15 minutes.

4 Stir in the kidney beans and cook for a further 5 minutes. Serve.

CHICKEN AND PEPPER CRACKERS

These hot and fiery chicken skewers are great for cooking on the barbecue or under the grill.

Serves 8 ■ Takes 25 minutes + marinating

16 long bamboo or metal skewers
4 x 150 g (5½ oz) skinless boneless
   chicken breasts, cut into bite
   size cubes
4 red peppers, de-seeded and cut
   into thick wedges
2 courgettes, cut on a diagonal into
   2.5 cm (1 inch) thick chunks
2 red onions, cut into wedges
2 corn on the cob, cut into 5 cm
   (2 inch) thick rounds
16, or more, bay leaves

For the marinade
150 g (5½ oz) low fat natural yogurt
2 red chillies, de-seeded and chopped
   finely
1 green chilli, de-seeded and chopped
   finely
zest and juice of 2 limes
6 tablespoons soy sauce
1 teaspoon Tabasco sauce
2 tablespoons Worcestershire sauce
1 teaspoon ground turmeric
2.5 cm (1 inch) piece of fresh root
   ginger, grated finely
2 garlic cloves, crushed
a small bunch of coriander, chopped

1 Mix all the marinade ingredients together in a large, shallow baking dish or oven tray.

2 If you are using bamboo skewers soak them in water for 30 minutes before using to prevent them burning. Thread the various bits of meat and vegetables with the bay leaves on to the skewers and then lay them in the marinade, basting to cover the meat.

3 Cover and leave to marinate for at least 30 minutes, but overnight in the fridge is best.

4 Preheat the grill or barbecue. Cook the skewers for 10 minutes, brushing them liberally with the marinade and turning often, until they are golden and charred at the edges and the chicken is cooked through.

GOOD IDEAS

Takeaway time

Instead of getting a takeaway, why not make your own? Home made versions taste just as good and are likely to be lower in fat. Get the whole family involved in cooking or setting the table and make a new, fun Friday night tradition.

CHICKEN TIKKA MASALA

Just right for a family Friday night in; serve with cooked brown rice.

Serves 4 ■ Takes 15 minutes to prepare + 30 minutes marinating, 20 minutes to cook

200 g (7 oz) low fat natural yogurt
2 teaspoons curry powder
2 teaspoons tomato purée
4 x 125 g (4½ oz) skinless boneless chicken breasts, diced
freshly ground black pepper

For the sauce
1 onion, chopped finely
low fat cooking spray
1 tablespoon curry powder
400 g can chopped tomatoes
150 ml (5 fl oz) chicken stock
2 tablespoons freshly chopped coriander

ROSEMARY LAMB BAKE

A one pot roast, ready in under an hour, is great for midweek suppers.

Serves 4 ■ Takes 15 minutes to prepare, 30 minutes to cook

400 g (14 oz) new potatoes, scrubbed and halved
400 g (14 oz) carrots, peeled and cut into chunks
2 red onions, cut into wedges
8 x 125 g (4½ oz) lamb leg steaks
4 rosemary sprigs
600 ml (1 pint) chicken or vegetable stock
freshly ground black pepper

1 Preheat the oven to Gas Mark 6/200°C/fan oven 180°C.
2 Place the potatoes, carrots and onions in a large roasting tin. Sprinkle with a little black pepper. Place the lamb steaks and rosemary on top.
3 Pour over the stock and bake for 30 minutes until golden and cooked through.

Tips You can use the same quantity of lean pork chops, trimmed of all fat, instead of the lamb.

For a change when using lamb or pork, add half a thinly sliced lemon to the vegetables – it will cook in the stock and give the juices extra flavour.

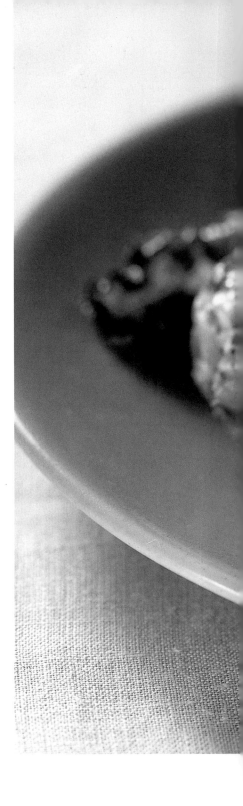

Eating together

Make sure the whole family sits at a table to eat as often as possible. Turn off the TV and make supper an event to look forward to by dressing the table up with fun, cheap, coloured plates or glasses. It will encourage children to eat new foods too.

TUNA CAKES WITH SPRING ONION SALSA

Serves 4 ■ Takes 35 minutes

400 g (14 oz) potatoes, peeled and diced
185 g can tuna chunks in spring water, drained and flaked roughly
1 teaspoon lemon juice
low fat cooking spray
freshly ground black pepper

For the salsa
4 spring onions, chopped finely
5 cm (2 inches) cucumber, seeds removed and flesh diced finely
1 teaspoon lemon juice

1 Bring a pan of water to the boil and cook the potatoes for 15–20 minutes, until tender.

2 While the potatoes are cooking, in a small bowl mix together all the salsa ingredients then leave to marinate.

3 When the potatoes are just cooked through, drain and mash them, then stir in the tuna and lemon juice and season with black pepper. Divide the mixture into eight and shape into small cakes.

4 Spray a large, non stick frying pan with the cooking spray and fry the cakes for 3 minutes. Then gently turn them over and cook for a further 2 minutes.

5 Serve two tuna cakes per person with a helping of salsa.

Sugar free
If you have soft drinks at meal times, switch to water. It's an easy change that will cut your sugar intake right down.

CARIBBEAN BBQ RUMP STEAKS

Colourful and tasty, this barbecued food will go down a treat.

Serves 4 ■ Takes 10 minutes to prepare, 10 minutes to cook

**4 x 150 g (5½ oz) beef rump
steaks, trimmed of all fat**
juice of a lime or ½ a lemon
1 teaspoon Jamaican jerk seasoning
2 red chillis, halved and de-seeded
2 courgettes, sliced diagonally
**1 red pepper, cored, de-seeded
and cut into six pieces**
**1 yellow pepper, cored, de-seeded
and cut into six pieces**
low fat cooking spray
4 fresh thyme sprigs
freshly ground black pepper

1 Preheat the barbecue, griddle pan or grill.
2 Brush the steaks with the lime or lemon juice, then sprinkle with the jerk seasoning. Cover and keep cool until ready to cook.
3 Spray the steaks, chillies, courgettes and peppers with the cooking spray and barbecue for 4–6 minutes, or until done to your liking, turning occasionally. If using a griddle pan or grill, you will need to cook the chillies, courgettes and peppers before cooking the steaks.
4 Serve, garnished with the thyme sprigs and seasoned with pepper.

Tip Simply press steaks with your finger to test that they are done – a rare steak will leave a slight indentation, a medium steak will be quite firm and a well-done steak will be firm. Check with a sharp knife if you're still unsure.

CHUNKY FISH FINGERS

Serves 4 ■ Takes 35 minutes ■ ❄ (fish fingers only)

8 x 15 g (½ oz) wholewheat
   crispbreads
4 x 100 g (3 ½ oz) skinless cod
   loin fillets, each cut into 2 or 3
   long fingers
1 egg, beaten
250 g (9 oz) frozen peas
½ x 25 g packet of fresh mint,
   leaves only

For the tartare sauce
juice of ½ a lemon
4 tablespoons Quark
1 tablespoon low fat natural yogurt
1 tablespoon chopped fresh dill
1 teaspoon capers, drained and
   chopped finely
25 g (1 oz) cocktail gherkins,
   chopped finely

1 Put the crispbreads into a food processor and whizz until fine crumbs or use a hand blender. Transfer to a shallow dish. Dip the cod pieces in the crumbs, coating them thoroughly. Dip the cod pieces into the beaten egg and then back into the crumbs, ensuring they are completely coated.
2 Preheat the grill to medium high and grill the fish fingers for 10 minutes, turning once halfway through.
3 Meanwhile, put the peas into a pan of boiling water and bring to the boil. Simmer for 3 minutes or until tender. Drain the peas and then whizz them in the food processor briefly with the mint leaves, until half puréed. Keep warm.
4 Mix together all the ingredients for the tartare sauce in a bowl and serve with the fish fingers and mushy peas.

SPICY PRAWN AND SPINACH CURRY

Serves 4 ■ Takes 25 minutes

low fat cooking spray
2.5 cm (1 inch) piece of fresh root
ginger, peeled and grated
2 garlic cloves, diced finely
2 onions, chopped finely
1 teaspoon cumin seeds
1 teaspoon coriander seeds
½ teaspoon ground turmeric
½ teaspoon each mustard seeds and
fennel seeds, ground in a pestle
and mortar or spice grinder
1 small red or green chilli, chopped
finely
100 ml (3½ fl oz) vegetable stock
400 g can chopped tomatoes
450 g (1 lb) fresh or frozen spinach,
defrosted
1 tablespoon soy sauce
450 g (1 lb) fresh or frozen peeled
prawns, defrosted
200 g (7 oz) low fat natural yogurt
bunch of fresh coriander

1 Spray a large, lidded, non stick frying pan or wok with the cooking spray and stir fry the ginger, garlic, onions, spices, seeds and chilli with the stock until the stock has boiled away and the onions are soft.

2 Add the tomatoes, spinach and soy sauce and allow to simmer for 10 minutes with a lid on.

3 Add the prawns and stir through. Simmer for 3–4 minutes, remove from the heat, stir in the yogurt and coriander and serve.

Serving suggestion Serve with 150 g (5½ oz) of cooked brown rice per person.

APPLE AND PORK BRAISE

Serves 4 ■ Takes 30 minutes to prepare, 25 minutes to cook

low fat cooking spray
400 g (14 oz) pork leg steaks,
trimmed of all fat and diced into
bite size pieces
2 small onions, chopped
2 garlic cloves, crushed
4 celery stalks, chopped finely
a small bunch of fresh sage, chopped,
but reserve a few small whole
leaves to garnish
450 g (1 lb) cooking apples, peeled,
cored and chopped
300 ml (½ pint) vegetable stock
freshly ground black pepper

1 Heat a large, lidded, non stick frying pan and spray with the cooking spray, then stir fry the pork for a few minutes until browned on all sides.

2 Add the onions and garlic and stir fry for another 5 minutes, until softened, adding a little water if necessary to prevent them from sticking.

3 Add the celery, sage, apples and stock and season with black pepper. Bring to the boil, then cover and simmer for 25 minutes. Serve garnished with the reserved sage leaves.

Tip To braise meat, place it in a large frying pan with a little low fat cooking spray on a low temperature. Fry the meat with any 'marinade' ingredients such as garlic and onion, allowing the meat to gently combine with the flavours. Add a little water or liquid and then simmer gently to draw out the flavours.

MANGO AND PASSION FRUIT FOOL

A ripe mango should feel just soft to the touch, and smell perfumed, while a ripe passion fruit should have a slightly dimpled skin, but feel fairly heavy, indicating that it is still full of juice.

Serves 4 ■ Takes 5 minutes ■

2 large ripe mangoes
2 x 150 g pots 0% fat Greek yogurt
4 passion fruit

1 Peel the mangoes using a vegetable peeler, then chop the flesh away from the central stones. Blend to a purée in a food processor, or using a hand held blender.
2 Mix in the yogurt until smooth then stir in the seeds and juice of two passion fruit. Divide between four glasses.
3 Spoon the seeds and juice of the remaining passion fruit on top of the fools before serving.

Tip You can eat the fool straightaway or it can be prepared in advance and chilled for up to 2 hours.

SPICY PEARS WITH APRICOT SAUCE

A little spice lifts the flavour of this fast fruity pudding, but if you don't have any nutmeg in the cupboard, you can use a little mixed spice or cinnamon instead.

Serves 4 ■ Takes 7 minutes ■

2 x 411 g cans pear quarters in
juice, drained
freshly grated nutmeg
2 x 210 g cans apricots in juice
8 tablespoons very low fat plain
fromage frais

1 Preheat a non stick frying pan and pat the pear quarters dry on kitchen paper. Add the pears to the pan and fry for 2 minutes either side until caramelised. Grate a little nutmeg over the pears as they cook.
2 Meanwhile, tip the apricots and their juice into a liquidiser and blend until smooth, or use a hand held blender. Pour into four bowls, add the pan-fried pears and top with the fromage frais and an extra grating of nutmeg.

Treat time

There is no need to exclude treats – foods that are high in calories, low in nutrition but taste good – but limit them to every now and again. Don't use them as rewards or punishment and don't use them in place of wholesome snacks.

weekend favourites

Weekends are a time for the whole family to try out their cooking skills. Get the children interested in cooking from a young age and invite family and friends round and surprise them with these delicious and wholesome recipes.

From ideas for Sunday lunch to family favourites and stunning recipes that are perfect for a supper party, there is something here for any weekend. There are also some delicious desserts everyone will love.

PORK ROAST WITH RATATOUILLE

Serves 4 ■ Takes 20 minutes to prepare,
1 hour to cook + 10 minutes resting

**450 g (1 lb) vine ripened tomatoes,
    quartered or halved depending
    on size**
2 red onions, cut into wedges
**1 red pepper and 1 yellow or orange
    pepper, de-seeded and cut into
    wedges**
4 garlic cloves, unpeeled
**2 large courgettes, halved
    lengthways and cut into chunks**
**2 dessert apples, cored and cut into
    thick wedges**
a few rosemary or thyme sprigs
4 tablespoons soy sauce
**1 kg (2 lb 4 oz) boneless shoulder
    joint of pork, trimmed of all fat**
200 ml (7 fl oz) vegetable stock
2 tablespoons Dijon mustard
**150 g (5½ oz) virtually fat free
    fromage frais**
freshly ground black pepper

1 Preheat the oven to Gas Mark 4
180°C/fan oven 160°C.
2 Place all the vegetables and
the apple and herbs in a large
baking tray, sprinkle with the
soy sauce and black pepper and
toss together.

3 Place the pork joint on top of
the vegetables and roast for
30 minutes. Toss the vegetables
around, turn the pork and roast for
another 30 minutes.
4 Remove from the oven and
place the pork on a carving board,
covered with a piece of foil for
10 minutes, to allow to rest.
Pour any fat off the vegetables,
placing them in a serving bowl
and keep warm.
5 Place the roasting tray on the
hob. Add the vegetable stock and
bring to the boil, scraping up stuck
on juices with a wooden spoon.
6 Add the mustard and stir in then
remove from the heat and stir in
the fromage frais. Serve the
sauce with the ratatouille and
carved meat.

ROAST VEGETABLE PILAFF

Serves 6 ■ Takes 20 minutes to prepare, 45 minutes to cook ■ Ⓨ

For the roast vegetables

500 g (1 lb 2 oz) parsnips, peeled and cut into wedges

300 g (10½ oz) carrots, peeled and chopped roughly

300 g (10½ oz) butternut or acorn squash, peeled, de-seeded and chopped roughly

6 shallots, halved

1 head of garlic, broken into whole cloves

1 tablespoon soy sauce

1 tablespoon balsamic vinegar

a few fresh rosemary sprigs, woody stems removed, chopped roughly and reserving one sprig for the garnish

low fat cooking spray

freshly ground black pepper

For the rice

300 g (10½ oz) dried brown rice

a pinch of saffron

850 ml (1½ pints) vegetable stock

1 Preheat the oven to Gas Mark 4/180°C/fan oven 160°C and place all the roast vegetable ingredients except the cooking spray and seasoning in a large roasting tin. Spray with the cooking spray, season with pepper, then toss together and spray again. Roast on the top shelf of the oven for 45 minutes or until tender.

2 Meanwhile, place the rice in a lidded ovenproof casserole. Stir the saffron into the stock, pour this over the rice and stir. Bring to the boil then stir well. Cover and cook in the oven on a lower shelf for 40 minutes.

3 Remove the casserole from the oven, stir in the roasted vegetables and then return the casserole to the oven for a further 5 minutes, or until the rice is tender. The pilaff should be slightly moist, so if the rice dries out too quickly add a little more stock or water. Garnish with a sprig of rosemary, if you wish.

GOOD IDEAS

Rice is nice
Children can be resistant to change. If your family is used to white rice it may be hard to get them to accept a change to brown rice. Start small by cooking half and half and gradually increasing the proportion of brown rice. It takes a little more effort but it will be worth it.

STUFFED BABY SQUASH

Serves 4 ■ Takes 15 minutes to prepare,
40 minutes to cook ⓥ ■ ❄ (filling only)

4 small squash, each weighing about
    350 g (12 oz)
150 g (5½ oz) dried quinoa, washed
low fat cooking spray
2 garlic cloves, crushed
150 g (5½ oz) mushrooms, sliced
¼ of a lemon
150 g low fat cottage cheese with
    onion and chives
1 tablespoon capers, drained and
    rinsed
small bunch of fresh parsley or basil,
    chopped
freshly ground black pepper

For the orange and tomato sauce
2 garlic cloves, crushed
1 onion, peeled and chopped finely
400 g tomato passata or 400 g
    can chopped tomatoes
zest of an orange

1 Preheat the oven to Gas Mark 5/190°C/fan oven 170°C. Pierce the squash in several places with the tip of a sharp knife. Bake for 30 minutes or until tender. Remove from the oven and leave until cool enough to handle.
2 Meanwhile, put the quinoa in a saucepan with double the amount of water. Bring to the boil and simmer for 15 minutes or until tender. Drain and place in a large bowl.
3 Heat a large, non stick frying pan and spray with the cooking spray. Stir fry the garlic for a minute, add the mushrooms and stir fry on a high heat for 3–4 minutes or until softened. Squeeze over the lemon, season with black pepper, then add to the bowl with the cooked quinoa.
4 Slice the top off each squash and put to one side, then scoop out the seeds from the squash and discard them. Scoop out some of the flesh from each, leaving enough for the squash to retain their shape. Chop the flesh and add to the quinoa and mushroom mixture.

5 Stir the cottage cheese, capers and parsley (or basil) into the quinoa and mushroom mixture.
6 Place the squashes in an ovenproof dish and spoon the mixture in. Bake for a further 20 minutes.
7 Meanwhile, make the sauce. Spray the non stick frying pan again and stir fry the garlic and onion for a few minutes or until the onion is soft. Add the passata (or tomatoes) and orange zest and simmer for 10 minutes or until thick. Season to taste with black pepper and serve with the squash.

Variation This filling also works with red peppers instead of the squash, especially the lovely long Italian ones. They do not need the first baking, just fill them as in step 5 and bake for 15 minutes.

BACON-WRAPPED CHICKEN BREASTS ON ROASTED SQUASH

Excellent served as a tasty, fuss-free meal for friends – or simply for your family.

Serves 4 ■ Takes 15 minutes to prepare, 40 minutes to cook

1 butternut squash, peeled, de-seeded and cut into chunks
12 shallots, halved
low fat cooking spray
1 teaspoon cumin seeds (optional)
8 large basil or sage leaves, plus 4 to garnish
4 x 150 g (5½ oz) skinless boneless chicken breasts
4 rashers lean back bacon
20 cherry tomatoes, on the vine
freshly ground black pepper

1 Preheat the oven to Gas Mark 6/200°C/fan oven 180°C.
2 Put the butternut squash into a roasting pan with the shallots. Spray with the cooking spray and sprinkle with cumin seeds, if using. Season with black pepper and roast for 15 minutes.
3 Place two sage or basil leaves on top of each chicken breast, then wrap a bacon rasher around each one, securing them with cocktail sticks.
4 Remove the roasting tin from the oven and turn the vegetables over. Arrange the chicken breasts on top. Return to the oven and roast for a further 25–30 minutes, adding the vine tomatoes 5 minutes before the end of cooking time. Check that the chicken is cooked, by using a sharp knife to pierce the thickest part – the juices should run clear. If there are traces of pink, cook for a little longer.
5 Serve, garnished with a few more sage or basil leaves.

Tip Try using two red or white onions, thickly sliced, instead of the shallots.

ITALIAN MEATBALLS

Serves 4 ■ Takes 20 minutes to prepare, 40 minutes to cook ■ ❋

350 g (12 oz) lean lamb mince with 10% fat or less
25 g (1 oz) fresh wholemeal breadcrumbs
1 small onion, chopped finely
1 garlic clove, crushed
1 teaspoon dried oregano
1 teaspoon dried basil
1 egg, beaten
400 g can chopped tomatoes
300 ml (½ pint) passata
1 lamb or beef stock cube
freshly ground black pepper
2 tablespoons torn fresh basil leaves, to garnish

1 Place the mince in a mixing bowl with the breadcrumbs, onion, garlic, dried herbs, egg and some pepper. Mix together thoroughly then shape the mixture into 16 small balls.

2 Heat a large, lidded, non stick frying pan and dry fry the meatballs for 2–3 minutes to lightly brown and seal on all sides. Add the chopped tomatoes and passata to the pan and crumble in the stock cube.

3 Bring to the boil, stirring, then cover. Reduce the heat and simmer for 30 minutes.

4 To serve, place four meatballs onto each of the four plates and divide the sauce between them. Scatter with the fresh basil and serve.

CHICKEN GOULASH WITH DUMPLINGS

The delicious light dumplings are made with cottage cheese and polenta. They are the perfect accompaniment to this delicious stew.

Serves 4 ■ Takes 25 minutes to prepare, 45 minutes to cook

For the dumplings
1 egg, beaten
250 g (9 oz) cottage cheese
50 g (1¾ oz) quick cook polenta
freshly ground black pepper

For the goulash
low fat cooking spray
4 x 150 g (5½oz) skinless boneless chicken breasts
1 onion, chopped finely
2 leeks, chopped
2 celery sticks, chopped
3 garlic cloves, crushed
2 tomatoes, chopped roughly
a small bunch of fresh thyme, tough stems removed and leaves and tender stems chopped
600 ml (1 pint) vegetable or chicken stock
1 bay leaf
1 teaspoon paprika

1 Make the dumplings first by stirring the egg into the cottage cheese and then gently folding in the polenta. Season with black pepper. Cover and chill for at least 20 minutes.
2 For the goulash, heat a large, lidded, flameproof casserole dish and spray with the cooking spray. Season the chicken with black pepper and fry on both sides until golden brown.
3 Add the onion, leeks, celery, garlic, tomatoes, thyme, stock and bay leaf. Bring to the boil and then simmer for 45 minutes.
4 Meanwhile, shape the dumpling mixture into eight golf-ball sized dumplings using wet hands to stop them sticking.
5 Stir the paprika into the stew and then gently place the dumplings on top. Cover and steam for a further 5–10 minutes. Remove the bay leaf and serve.

family favourites

As a working mum with two children aged nine and 12, and a husband who works long hours, I have to stay one step ahead. If I didn't plan, we'd end up eating cheese on toast every night. But at the weekend, when there's more time to relax, everyone gets involved in the cooking. Since we made the decision to make ours a healthy-weight home, I insisted my husband Mark pitch in and help in the kitchen. Now that we are less reliant on ready-made meals he has to do his share; he has gradually developed his own repertoire of favourite recipes – he's up to 10 now and adding more all the time.

Sometimes my daughter Megan takes control of meals at the weekend; she's done food tech at school now and likes to make her own fish cakes and pasta tuna bake. When friends come round for Sunday lunch we might have Roast Pork with Ratatouille (page 96) or Moussaka (page 110) and no one ever has any idea that they are eating healthy, low-calorie, low-fat, low-salt dishes.

Michelle Ashwell, mum to Megan and Dominic

ROAST SALMON FILLETS WITH TANGY TOMATO CRUST

These crisp, tangy fillets are an easy supper. Serve with steamed broccoli.

Serves 4 ■ Takes 35 minutes

2 egg whites
1 tablespoon tomato purée
4 x 150 g (5½ oz) salmon fillets
100 g (3½ oz) fresh wholemeal breadcrumbs
low fat cooking spray
200 g (7 oz) cherry tomatoes, halved
a large bunch of basil or coriander, chopped (optional)
1 teaspoon balsamic vinegar
freshly ground black pepper

1 Preheat the oven to Gas Mark 6/200°C/fan oven 180°C.
2 Beat the egg whites with the tomato purée and pepper. Dip the fish fillets in the egg mixture first and then in the breadcrumbs to coat.
3 Place the coated fish on a baking tray sprayed with the cooking spray and bake for 25 minutes.
4 Meanwhile, place the cherry tomatoes, basil or coriander, if using, balsamic vinegar and a little black pepper in a small saucepan with 50 ml (2 fl oz) warm water. Cook over a low heat, stirring until the tomatoes start to break down.
5 Serve the fish with the sauce spooned over.

MOUSSAKA

Serve this flavoursome classic Greek dish with a crisp green salad.

Serves 4 ■ Takes 35 minutes to prepare, 40 minutes to cook

low fat cooking spray
500 g (1 lb 2 oz) lean lamb mince with 10% fat or less
1 onion, chopped finely
½ teaspoon dried mint
1 teaspoon cinnamon
500 g carton passata
1 aubergine, cut into 1 cm (½ inch) slices
500 g (1 lb 2 oz) potatoes, peeled and cut into 1 cm (½ inch) slices
1 egg, beaten
300 g (10½ oz) 0% fat Greek yogurt
freshly grated nutmeg
4 tomatoes, sliced
freshly ground black pepper

1 Preheat the grill. Heat a large, lidded saucepan, spray with the cooking spray and brown the lamb mince and onion for about 7 minutes, stirring to break up the meat.
2 Mix in the mint, cinnamon and passata. Season with black pepper, then cover and simmer for 5 minutes.
3 Mist the aubergine slices with the cooking spray and grill for 2–3 minutes on each side, until golden.
4 Preheat the oven to Gas Mark 6/200°C/ fan oven 180°C.
5 Add the potato slices to a large pan of boiling water, stirring gently so that they don't stick together. Simmer for 3–4 minutes, until tender but not falling apart, then drain carefully.
6 Spoon half the meat into a baking dish, then cover with half the potatoes. Repeat the meat and potato layers, then cover with the aubergines.
7 Mix the egg into the yogurt and add nutmeg and pepper to taste. Spread over the aubergines, then arrange the tomato slices on top.
8 Bake in the oven for 40 minutes until browned and bubbling.

FISH AND CHIPS

A crunchy, polenta-herb batter puts this great British speciality back on the menu.

Serves 4 ■ Takes 20 minutes to prepare, 35 minutes to cook

low fat cooking spray
2 large potatoes, peeled and cut into wedges
2 tablespoons malt vinegar
100 g (3½ oz) dried polenta, plus an extra 2 tablespoons
1 egg, beaten
120 ml (4 fl oz) skimmed milk
finely grated zest from a lemon
1 teaspoon dried mixed herbs
4 x 150 g (5½ oz) cod fillets
freshly ground black pepper

1 Preheat the oven to Gas Mark 6/200°C/fan oven 180°C. Coat two large baking trays with the cooking spray.
2 Place the potatoes in a large bowl and add the vinegar and pepper. Toss to coat. Arrange them on one of the prepared baking trays. Transfer to the oven and bake for 20 minutes.
3 Meanwhile, in a mixing bowl, combine the polenta, egg, milk, lemon zest, herbs and a little more pepper. Mix well to make a thick batter. Dust the fish with the 2 tablespoons of polenta. Place in the batter and turn to coat both sides. Place the fish on the second prepared baking tray and spoon over any remaining batter, patting it over the fish to make an even coating.
4 Transfer to the oven to bake with the potatoes for a further 18–20 minutes, until the potatoes and fish are cooked through and the polenta batter just starts to crack.

CABBAGE PARCELS WITH A SPICY RICE AND MUSHROOM FILLING
Spice up cabbage with this recipe.

Serves 4 ■ Takes 15 minutes to prepare, 20 minutes to cook ■ ⓥ

8 large cabbage leaves
low fat cooking spray
1 small onion, chopped finely
75 g (2¾ oz) mushrooms,
  chopped finely
½ teaspoon ground allspice
125 g (4½ oz) cooked brown rice
300 ml (½ pint) vegetable stock
freshly ground black pepper

For the quick tomato sauce
1 small onion, grated
1 garlic clove, crushed
400 g can chopped tomatoes
1 teaspoon dried oregano

1 Bring a pan of water to the boil and blanch the cabbage leaves for 1 minute, then drain and refresh under cold running water. Set aside on kitchen paper whilst you prepare the filling.
2 Heat a non stick pan, spray with the cooking spray and gently cook the onion, until soft. Add the mushrooms and cook for a further 3–4 minutes. Stir in the allspice and rice and season with pepper. Spoon equal amounts of the filling on to each leaf and roll them up, tucking in the ends to form neat parcels.

3 Place the parcels in the base of a large saucepan and pour over the stock. Cover and simmer gently for 20 minutes.
4 Meanwhile, prepare the tomato sauce. Put all the ingredients in a small pan and simmer for 15 minutes. Season with pepper.

5 To serve, remove the hot parcels with a slotted spoon and arrange two on each plate, with a little tomato sauce spooned alongside.

TURKEY AND VEGETABLE CASSEROLE

A lovely, warming winter dish, ideal for feeding the whole family.

Serves 4 ■ Takes 25 minutes to prepare, 50 minutes to cook

low fat cooking spray
1 large onion, sliced
450 g (1 lb) skinless boneless turkey breast, cut into bite size pieces
1 fennel bulb, sliced
2 carrots, peeled and sliced
1 leek, sliced
350 g (12 oz) butternut squash, peeled and sliced
450 g (1 lb) potatoes, peeled and sliced
600 ml (1 pint) chicken stock
1 tablespoon Worcestershire sauce
freshly ground black pepper

1 Preheat the oven to Gas Mark 6/200°C/fan oven 180°C.
2 Heat a frying pan and spray with the cooking spray. Cook the onion for 4–5 minutes. Remove from the pan and place in a deep, lidded casserole dish.
3 Spray the pan again with the cooking spray and cook the turkey meat until browned on all sides. Place this in the casserole dish on top of the onion.
4 Layer the remaining vegetables over the turkey, ending with a layer of potatoes on the top.

5 Mix together the stock and Worcestershire sauce and pour over the casserole. Season well with black pepper, cover with a lid and cook for 40–50 minutes.

POTATO AND HAM BAKE

This simple dish of baked sliced potatoes with ham and stock makes a wonderful family meal.

Serves 4 ■ Takes 15 minutes to prepare, 60 minutes to cook + 10 minutes standing

1 kg (9 oz) potatoes
2 onions, sliced thinly
200 g (7 oz) lean cooked ham, cut into thin slices
2 teaspoons cumin seeds
leaves from 4 thyme sprigs
800 ml (28 fl oz) fresh chicken or vegetable stock
freshly ground black pepper

1 Wash the potatoes well, pat dry then slice thinly either in a food processor or by hand.
2 Preheat the oven to Gas Mark 5/190°C/fan oven 170°C. Layer the potatoes, onions and ham together and place in a medium size, shallow, ovenproof dish, keeping some of the ham to sprinkle over the top together with the cumin, thyme leaves and pepper.

3 Pour over the stock and press the potatoes, onions and ham down under the stock. Cover with foil and bake for 30 minutes.
4 Remove the dish from the oven, uncover and return to the oven to brown and crisp the top for another 30 minutes. Stand for 10 minutes before serving.

Help yourselves
Let older children serve themselves and let all your children decide how much they want to eat.

SPAGHETTI BOLOGNESE

Serves 4 ■ Takes 20 minutes to prepare, 50 minutes to cook ■ ❋

low fat cooking spray
1 red onion, chopped finely
1 garlic clove, crushed
**225 g (8 oz) extra lean beef mince
   with 7% fat or less**
2 rashers lean back bacon, diced
2 celery stalks, trimmed and sliced
1 carrot, chopped finely
**150 g (5½ oz) button mushrooms,
   wiped and diced**
1 teaspoon dried mixed herbs
400 ml (14 fl oz) beef stock
2 tablespoons tomato purée
400 g (14 oz) can chopped tomatoes
**225 g (8 oz) dried wholewheat
   spaghetti**
**2 tablespoons chopped fresh parsley
   (optional)**
freshly ground black pepper

1 Heat a large frying pan and spray with the cooking spray. Cook the onion and garlic until softened. Add the mince and bacon and cook for a further 5 minutes until evenly browned.
2 Stir in the celery, carrot, mushrooms and herbs and cook for 2 minutes.
3 Pour the stock into the pan with the tomato purée and chopped tomatoes. Stir well, season to taste with black pepper and bring to the boil. Simmer for 50 minutes.

4 About 10 minutes before the bolognese is ready, bring a large pan of water to the boil. Cook the spaghetti according to the packet instructions until tender. Drain and toss with the chopped parsley, if using.
5 Divide the spaghetti between four warmed serving plates and top with the bolognese sauce to serve.

BAKED TUNA NIÇOISE

Enjoy a hot new take on a summer favourite to enjoy at any time of the year.

Serves 4 ■ Takes 15 minutes to prepare, 40 minutes to cook

**500 g (1 lb 2 oz) potatoes, peeled and
   cut into chunks**
low fat cooking spray
1 large red onion, sliced
**150 g (5½ oz) green beans, topped
   and tailed**
12 stoned black olives, in brine
4 large tomatoes, quartered
4 x 125 g (17½ oz) tuna steaks
2 tablespoons lemon juice
2 tablespoons capers
freshly ground black pepper
**2 tablespoons fresh chopped parsley,
   to garnish**

1 Preheat the oven to Gas Mark 6/200°C/fan oven 180°C.

2 Put the potatoes into a roasting pan and spray with the cooking spray, tossing to coat. Transfer to the oven and bake for 20 minutes.

3 Add the red onion and green beans to the potatoes, stir well, then bake for a further 10 minutes. Remove the roasting pan from the oven.

4 Stir the potato mixture and add the olives and tomatoes. Arrange the tuna steaks on top. Sprinkle the lemon juice and capers over them and season with black pepper. Return to the oven and bake for a further 8–10 minutes.

5 Serve, scattered with plenty of chopped fresh parsley.

Tip If you prefer, use firm white fish instead of tuna, such as halibut or sea bass.

GRILLED MIXED BERRIES WITH VANILLA CUSTARD SAUCE

Grilling the berries in this simple yet elegant dessert helps release their sweet juices.

Serves 4 ■ Takes 20 minutes ■ ⓨ

100 g (3½ oz) strawberries
100 g (3½ oz) blueberries
100 g (3½ oz) raspberries
2 tablespoons artificial sweetener
1 tablespoon lemon juice
125 g (4½ oz) regular silken tofu
4 tablespoons skimmed milk
1 teaspoon vanilla essence

1 Preheat the grill to high.
2 Place the berries in a medium sized bowl and toss with half the sweetener and the lemon juice. Spcon into a shallow, ovenproof baking dish large enough to hold all the berries in a single layer. Place the dish 3–4 inches from the grill and cook until the fruit just starts to ourst, about 5 minutes. Remove from the grill and set aside.
3 Combine the tofu, milk, vanilla essence and remaining sweetener in a blender or bowl and blend until smooth, about 2–3 minutes.
4 To serve, divide the berries between four shallow bowls and top with vanilla sauce.

Tip The sauce can be stored, covered, for up to 5 days in the refrigerator.

FROZEN FRUIT SALAD
You will need two 12 hole ice cube trays for this recipe.

Serves 4 ■ Takes 15 minutes + 4 hours freezing ■ ⓨ

200 g (7 oz) fresh raspberries
2 teaspoons granulated artificial sweetener
zest of ½ an orange
200 g (7 oz) kiwi, peeled and chopped
juice of a lime
200 g (7 oz) cantaloupe melon, de-seeded, peeled and cubed
1 ripe mango, peeled, stoned and sliced
150 g (5½ oz) fresh strawberries, hulled and quartered

1 Whizz the raspberries in a food processor or with a hand blender until puréed, and then pass through a sieve. Sweeten the purée with 1 teaspoon of artificial sweetener and add the orange zest. Pour into six ice cube tray holes.
2 Whizz the kiwi until puréed. Sweeten with 1 teaspoon of artificial sweetener and add the juice of 1 lime. Pour into another six ice cube tray holes.
3 Whizz the melon until puréed and pour into yet another six ice cube tray holes. Freeze all the ice cube trays for 4 hours or overnight until frozen.

4 Empty the ice cubes into a large bowl and toss with the mango and strawberries. Serve immediately.

Slow cooking

6 For me the best invention ever is the slow cooker. I put all the ingredients in before we go out, switch it on and leave it to work its magic.

When you come home starving, that's the danger point, when you think: 'Oh, I'm too tired to cook, let's pick up a pizza.' But instead, thanks to the slow cooker, when I open the door in the evening and that delicious smell hits me, I think: 'Mmmm, supper's ready.'
It's an ideal way to cook Chicken Goulash with Dumplings (page 105). I make the dumplings beforehand and add them for the last 10 minutes while we get changed and set the table.
Turkey and Vegetable Casserole (page 112) is another good one for the slow cooker.
I also use mine to do baked potatoes for a quick supper in the week – just add baked beans or a salad and you're done. *Michelle Ashwell*

teenage cooks

Kids love cooking, so take a break and encourage them into the kitchen with these fun recipes. They are more likely to eat wholesome meals if they have cooked them first too.

There are lots of ideas here for teenagers to try. Some are wholesome variations on typical teenage favourites like chicken korma and scampi and chips, and others are just simply great fun to put together.

SPAGHETTI NAPOLI

A classic thick tomato sauce for pasta. Serve with a green salad of interesting fresh leaves like rocket, cos, chicory and oakleaf with cucumber, radishes and sugar snap peas. Sprinkle over a squeeze of lemon juice and some pepper.

Serves 4 ■ Takes 30 minutes
■ ❷ ■ ❅ (sauce only)

350 g (12 oz) dried wholewheat spaghetti
low fat cooking spray
1 large onion, chopped
2 garlic cloves, crushed
2 x 400 g cans chopped tomatoes
200 g (7 oz) cherry tomatoes, halved
1 teaspoon artificial sweetener
1 teaspoon dried oregano
a small bunch of fresh parsley or basil (optional)
freshly ground black pepper

1 Bring a pan of water to the boil and cook the pasta according to the packet instructions until tender.
2 Meanwhile, spray a large, non stick frying pan with the cooking spray and fry the onion and garlic for about 5 minutes until softened, adding a few tablespoons of water if they begin to stick.

3 Add the chopped tomatoes and cherry tomatoes, sweetener, oregano and pepper. Stir together and bring to the boil, and then simmer for 15–20 minutes until thick.
4 Drain the pasta and add it to the sauce along with 4 tablespoons of the cooking water. Stir together until the pasta is well coated with the sauce. Serve sprinkled with fresh herbs, if using.

CHICKEN SCHNITZEL

Have fun by bashing out these chicken breasts with a meat mallet or rolling pin. Serve with a salad or lightly cooked fresh vegetables.

Serves 4 ■ Takes 15 minutes to prepare, 25 minutes to cook

low fat cooking spray
125 g (4½ oz) dried couscous
200 ml (⅓ pint) hot chicken stock
4 x 150 g (5½ oz) skinless boneless chicken breasts
100 g (3½ oz) low fat soft cheese
2 spring onions, chopped finely
1 red chilli, de-seeded and chopped finely (optional)
4 thin slices lean ham
1 egg
freshly ground black pepper

1 Preheat the oven to Gas Mark 5/190°C/fan oven 170°C. Spray a baking sheet with the cooking spray.
2 Put the couscous into a heatproof bowl. Pour the stock over the couscous, cover with clingfilm and leave to swell and cool for 10–15 minutes.
3 Meanwhile, place the chicken breasts, well spaced, on a large piece of clingfilm. Cover with a second piece of clingfilm. Using a meat mallet or rolling pin, gently but firmly beat out the chicken breasts until they are about half their original thickness.
4 Mix together the soft cheese, spring onions and chilli, if using. Season with black pepper. Spread this mixture over one side of each chicken breast, then cover with a slice of ham, trimming it to fit.
5 Beat the egg with 2 tablespoons of cold water. Brush the ham and chicken with beaten egg, then coat in the cooled couscous. Arrange on the prepared baking sheet.
6 Bake in the oven for 20–25 minutes, until the chicken is tender. Check with a sharp knife inserted into the thickest part – the juices should run clear.

Tip You could use bulgar wheat instead of couscous, though the texture of the coating will be a little grainier.

GOOD IDEAS

Learning to cook

If you have teenagers who are reluctant to cook, start small by encouraging them to put together foods that need no cooking, such as salads. Once they are more confident in the kitchen they can move on to simple recipes.

CHINESE SPICE-RUBBED PORK WITH STIR FRY VEGETABLES

Serve this delicious dish in the spirit of Chinese New Year. Roll pork fillet in Chinese spices to give it a great flavour, then serve with a stir fry.

Serves 4 ■ Takes 15 minutes to prepare, 10 minutes to cook

1 teaspoon Chinese 5 spice powder
1 teaspoon ground coriander
1 teaspoon chilli powder
zest and juice from ½ a lemon
500 g (1 lb 2 oz) pork tenderloin, trimmed of all fat
125 g (4½ oz) egg noodles
low fat cooking spray
1 spring onion, chopped
1 red, green or yellow pepper, de-seeded and chopped
140 g (5 oz) mange tout
2 celery sticks, chopped
1 teaspoon fresh root ginger, peeled and grated
2 tablespoons soy sauce

1 Sprinkle the Chinese 5 spice powder, coriander, chilli powder and lemon zest onto a plate. Roll the whole pork fillet in this mixture and then slice into 1 cm (½ inch) pieces.

2 Place the noodles in a large bowl and cover with boiling water. Soak for 4–6 minutes, or according to the packet instructions. Drain thoroughly.

3 Meanwhile, heat a wok or large frying pan and spray with the cooking spray. Cook the pork slices for 5–6 minutes, turning to cook both sides. Remove from the pan and keep warm.

4 Add all the vegetables and ginger to the wok or frying pan and stir fry for 3–4 minutes. Add the noodles with the lemon juice and soy sauce, reheat for a few moments, then serve with the pork.

Variation Use 2 teaspoons of Chinese 5 spice powder and omit the coriander or chilli powder, if you like.

CHICKEN KORMA

Forget the takeaway menu and make this for the family instead.

Serves 4 ■ Takes 15 minutes to prepare, 50 minutes to cook

low fat cooking spray
2 onions, chopped
1 apple, peeled, cored and chopped
4 teaspoons curry powder
450 g (1 lb) skinless boneless chicken breast, cut into bite size pieces
½ pint chicken stock
25 g (1 oz) sultanas
1 tablespoon tomato purée
125 g (4½ oz) dried brown basmati rice
1 banana, sliced
4 fresh coriander sprigs, chopped finely
8 tablespoons low fat natural yogurt
freshly ground black pepper

1 Spray a large, lidded saucepan with the cooking spray. Sauté the onions and apple for 3–4 minutes, until the chicken is sealed all over. Stir in the curry powder and add the chicken. Cook, stirring, for 2–3 minutes, until sealed all over.
2 Add the stock, sultanas and tomato purée. Bring to the boil. Reduce the heat, cover and simmer gently for about 40 minutes.

3 After 20 minutes, bring a pan of water to the boil, add the rice and cook according to the packet instructions. Drain.
4 Just before serving, add the sliced banana, chopped coriander and 4 tablespoons of yogurt to the curry. Season with black pepper and cook for 2 minutes.
5 Serve the curry with the rice, adding one tablespoon of yogurt to each portion.

PRAWN AND SPRING ONION SKEWERS WITH CREAMY PEPPER SAUCE

Grilled red pepper, spring onion and lemon transform into a colourful, flavourful dipping sauce for prawns.

Serves 6 ■ Takes 25 minutes to prepare, 15 minutes to cook

1 red pepper, de-seeded and quartered
low fat cooking spray
60 g (2 oz) fresh parsley
8 spring onions, 1 chopped and the remainder sliced into 6 pieces each
100 ml (3½ fl oz) low fat natural yogurt
zest and juice of ½ a lemon
1 garlic clove
36 raw king prawns, peeled
freshly ground black pepper

1 Preheat the grill to medium high. Coat the pepper with the cooking spray. Grill, turning as needed, until lightly charred and tender, about 10–15 minutes.
2 To make the sauce, place the grilled pepper, parsley, 1 chopped spring onion, yogurt, lemon zest, lemon juice and garlic in a food processor. Pulse until the mixture is blended and ingredients are finely chopped. Set aside.
3 Alternately thread three prawns and three pieces of spring onion onto each of 12 metal or wooden skewers. Lightly spray with the cooking spray and season with black pepper.
4 Grill the skewers, turning once, until the prawns are just cooked through and have turned pink, about 2–4 minutes. Serve two skewers and about 2 tablespoons of sauce per serving.

Tip If you're using wooden skewers, soak them in water for 30 minutes before use to prevent charring.

SPICY STEAK TACOS

Enjoy these tasty tacos for a quick light bite – they only take minutes to make.

Serves 4 ■ Takes 10 minutes to prepare, 4 minutes to cook

1 **Little Gem lettuce, shredded**
2 **spring onions, chopped**
4 **radishes, sliced finely**
1 **large tomato, diced**
¼ **cucumber, diced**
juice of ½ a lemon
2 **teaspoons Cajun seasoning**
200 g (5½ oz) **beef rump steak, trimmed of all fat**
low fat cooking spray
4 **corn tortillas**

1 Preheat the oven to Gas Mark 4/180°C/fan oven 160°C
2 Mix together the lettuce, spring onions, radishes, tomato and cucumber. Sprinkle with the lemon juice.
3 Rub the Cajun seasoning into the steak, then slice it thinly. Heat a non stick frying pan and spray with the cooking spray. Fry the steak strips for 3–4 minutes or until done to your liking.
4 Meanwhile, shape the tortillas over an oven rack and bake in the oven for a few minutes until crisp.
5 Divide the salad and hot steak between the baked tortillas. Serve at once.

CHICKEN NOODLES

A quick dish that is delicious without the chicken too.

Serves 4 ■ Takes 15 minutes to prepare, 15 minutes to cook

200 g (7 oz) dried rice noodles
low fat cooking spray
a bunch of spring onions, sliced
4 garlic cloves, sliced thinly
200 g (7 oz) skinless boneless
   chicken breast, sliced thinly
150 g (5½ oz) beansprouts
2 large carrots, sliced into
   matchsticks
150 g (5½ oz) mange tout, sliced
   thinly
1 red pepper, de-seeded and sliced
   finely
4 tablespoons soy sauce
1 tablespoon Worcestershire sauce
100 ml (3½ fl oz) vegetable or
   chicken stock
2 limes

1 Soak the rice noodles in boiling water as directed on the packet. Drain thoroughly.

2 Spray a large, non stick frying pan or wok with the cooking spray and stir fry the spring onions and garlic for 1–2 minutes, adding a tablespoon of water if necessary to stop them sticking. Add the chicken and stir fry for a few minutes, until browned all over.

3 Add all the other ingredients, including the noodles (except the limes) and stir fry for a final few minutes, tossing together to mix everything well.

4 Squeeze over the juice of one lime and cut the other into wedges. Serve the noodles with the lime wedges.

SCAMPI AND CHIPS

Serves 4 ■ Takes 15 minutes to prepare,
40 minutes to cook

**700 g (1 lb 9 oz) potatoes, cut into
    wedges**
low fat cooking spray
**450 g (1 lb) raw peeled prawns,
    thawed if frozen**
1 egg
75 g (2¾ oz) dried polenta
1 teaspoon dried mixed herbs
6 tablespoons 0% fat Greek yogurt
1 tablespoon capers, chopped finely
**15 g (½ oz) pickled gherkins,
    chopped finely**
freshly ground black pepper
1 lemon, cut into 4 wedges, to serve

1 Preheat the oven to Gas Mark
6/200°C/fan oven 180°C.
2 Put the potato wedges into a
roasting tray and spray with the
cooking spray. Season with black
pepper and roast for 30 minutes.
3 Pat the prawns dry with
kitchen paper. Beat the egg with
2 tablespoons of cold water.
Sprinkle the polenta onto a plate
and mix with the dried herbs and
some black pepper.
4 Dip the prawns in the beaten
egg, then roll them in the polenta
mixture. Place on a non stick
baking tray and bake in the oven
with the potato wedges for the last
10 minutes.

5 Mix together the yogurt, capers
and gherkins. Serve with the
scampi and chips, with wedges of
lemon on the side.

Tips Use 75 g (2¾oz) of fresh
wholemeal breadcrumbs instead
of instant polenta, if you prefer.

Traditionally, Dublin Bay prawns
or langoustines are used. These
are expensive, so use large
prawns instead.

CHICK PEA AND VEGETABLE PATTIES WITH CORIANDER TOMATO SALSA

Serves 4 ■ Takes 10 minutes to prepare,
30 minutes to cook ■ Ⓥ

low fat cooking spray
**400 g can chick peas, drained
    and rinsed**
200 g (7 oz) plain tofu
1 carrot, grated
1 courgette, grated
25 g (1 oz) sweetcorn
½ teaspoon cumin seeds
½ teaspoon ground coriander
**2 tablespoons chopped fresh
    coriander**
1 egg, separated
2 large tomatoes, chopped finely
¼ cucumber, chopped finely
freshly ground black pepper

1 Preheat the oven to Gas Mark
4/180°C/fan oven 160°C.
Spray a baking sheet with the
cooking spray.
2 Put the chick peas and tofu into
a blender or food processor and
blend for 15–20 seconds, until
combined, though not too smooth.
Turn out into a bowl and add the
carrot, courgette, sweetcorn,
cumin seeds, ground coriander
and 1 tablespoon of coriander.
Add the egg yolk and some black
pepper. Mix together thoroughly,
then form into eight patties.
3 Beat the egg white with
1 tablespoon of water. Brush over
the patties, then arrange them on
the baking sheet. Bake for
25–30 minutes.
4 Meanwhile, make the salsa by
mixing together the tomatoes,
cucumber and remaining
coriander. Season with black
pepper. Serve with the patties.

FRAGRANT LAMB CURRY

This gorgeous curry keeps well in the fridge for a few days or can be made in advance and frozen.

Serves 4 ■ Takes 10 minutes to prepare, 1 hour to cook ■ ❄

low fat cooking spray
350 g (12 oz) lean lamb, trimmed of all fat and cut into bite size pieces
2 large onions, sliced finely
4 garlic cloves, crushed
2 teaspoons curry powder
1 teaspoon garam masala
450 g (1 lb) vegetables (such as cauliflower and carrot)
300 ml (½ pint) vegetable stock
150 ml (¼ pint) very low fat natural yogurt
freshly ground black pepper
a small bunch of fresh coriander, chopped, to garnish (optional)

1 Heat a large, lidded, non stick frying pan and spray with the cooking spray. Season the lamb with pepper and stir fry for 5 minutes, or until browned all over.
2 Add the onions and garlic and stir fry for 5 minutes more, adding a little water to prevent them from sticking and to help them soften. Add the curry powder anc garam masala and cook for a further 2 minutes.

3 Add the vegetables and stock. Bring to the boil then cover and simmer for 15 minutes. Remove the lid and simmer for a further 30 minutes or until the sauce has thickened.
4 Remove from the heat and allow to cool a little, then stir in the yogurt and fresh coriander, if using, and serve.

BROTH FONDUE

If you have a fondue set this is a good opportunity to get it out. The idea is that your family put skewers of meat and chunks of vegetables into a large pot of simmering broth then dip them into little dishes of soy sauce.

Serves 4 ■ Takes 15 minutes to prepare, 5 minutes to cook

500 g (1 lb 2 oz) skinless boneless chicken breast or lean beef steak cut into bite size pieces
3 tablespoons low salt soy sauce
800 ml (1½ pints) chicken stock
1 courgette, cut into bite size pieces
1 red, green or yellow pepper, de-seeded and cut into bite size pieces
100 g (3½ oz) baby sweetcorn
100 g (3½ oz) mushrooms
125 g (4½ oz) asparagus spears
200 g (7 oz) baby new potatoes, cooked
8 raw king or tiger prawns

low salt soy sauce, for dipping
3 spring onions, chopped roughly
3 fresh coriander sprigs

1 Mix the chicken or beef with the soy sauce and leave to marinate for 10 minutes.
2 Put the stock in a saucepan and bring to a boil. When boiling, pour into a fondue pot with the burner lit underneath. Adjust the flame so the broth gently simmers.
3 Lay the chicken or beef, vegetables and prawns out attractively on a platter with long wooden skewers on the side. Pour the soy sauce for dipping into small dishes. Add the spring onions and coriander to the broth.
4 Your guests can then skewer a piece of chicken or beef, and one or two vegetables or a prawn onto a skewer then pop it into the simmering broth. The meat should take about 2–3 minutes to cook and can be dipped lightly into the soy sauce.
5 When all the meat and vegetables are eaten, pour the (by now) very tasty broth into cups for soup.

teen spirit

'I've got five children: two are teenagers – Ross, 16, and Ryan, 14 – and the two girls (Georgia, 11, and Lana, 12) are coming up to their teens. Then there's Louis, who's not that far off, aged eight. After years of being told to be careful of hot pans and sharp knives they adore having free rein in the kitchen and love it now they're actually allowed to cook. 'Oh great, is it my turn?' is a phrase I'll never get tired of hearing.

School holidays are an ideal opportunity for them to cook. They go through the recipe books, make a list, then go shopping. Then they do everything from chopping and cooking to dishing up. The boys often cook together and are very good on presentation, doing a three-course meal with homemade tomato soup to start and finishing with individual fruit salads in wine glasses.

Teenagers these days have far more sophisticated tastes. If I serve them meat and two veg, they're likely to go: 'Urgh.' But if I rustle up a stir fry, they are much more enthusiastic, so it makes sense to get them into the kitchen with recipes like Chinese Spice-Rubbed Pork with Stir Fry Vegetables (page 124) or Chick Pea and Vegetable Patties with Coriander Tomato Salsa (page 130) or Prawn and Spring Onion Skewers with Creamy Pepper Sauce (page 126), as well as old favourites like Spaghetti Napoli (page 122), which is great if they have vegetarian friends round for supper. I know that when they eventually leave home, they've got the foundations of making healthy food choices, as well as the confidence to cook for themselves.

Deborah Court, mum to Ross, Ryan, Georgia, Lana and Louis

Take care

Putting food on skewers is great fun. Do it as a whole family and choose whatever vegetables are in season. You can skewer and grill fruit too – just make sure everyone is careful with the sharp skewers.

GINGERED PORK, PINEAPPLE AND PEPPER SKEWERS

Cubes of pork tenderloin are marinated in soy and ginger, skewered with juicy pineapple and sweet red pepper chunks and then grilled to perfection.

Serves 4 ■ Takes 20 minutes to prepare, 10 minutes to cook + marinating

2 tablespoons soy sauce
1 teaspoon grated fresh ginger root
1 garlic clove, crushed
225 g (8 oz) canned pineapple,
    drained and cut into chunks
225 g (8 oz) pork tenderloin, trimmed
    of all fat and cut into chunks
1 red, green or yellow pepper,
    de-seeded and cut into chunks
low fat cooking spray
240 g (8½ oz) dried couscous
25 g (1 oz) spring onions

1 In a resealable food storage bag, combine the soy sauce, ginger and garlic. Finely chop two pineapple chunks and add to the bag. Add the pork, seal the bag and gently shake to coat in the marinade. Refrigerate for at least 30 minutes or up to 4 hours.

2 Preheat the grill to medium high. Remove the pork from the marinade. Alternately thread two pieces of pork, two pieces of pepper and two pieces of pineapple onto each of the eight wooden skewers. Spray with the cooking spray.

3 Grill the skewers, turning once, until the pork is cooked in the centre and the pepper and pineapple are lightly charred and tender, about 6–8 minutes. Remove from the heat.

4 Meanwhile, in a bowl, pour 400 ml (14 fl oz) hot water over the couscous, stir once and then cover and leave to stand for 5 minutes until the couscous has absorbed the liquid.

5 Fluff up the couscous and combine with the spring onions. Serve two skewers and a portion of the couscous each.

COD PARCELS WITH LEMON AND DILL SAUCE

This is a lovely, easy way to cook fish as the flavours are sealed in during cooking and each person opens their own parcel. The lemon and dill sauce also goes well with plain grilled fillets of fish, chicken breasts.

Serves 4 ■ Takes 25 minutes

1 fennel bulb, sliced finely
4 x 150 g (5½ oz) cod steaks
zest and juice of a lemon
freshly ground black pepper

For the sauce
low fat cooking spray
2 shallots, sliced finely
zest and juice of a lemon
a small bunch of dill, chopped finely
6 tablespoons virtually fat free
    fromage frais

1 Preheat the oven to Gas Mark 6/200°C/fan oven 180°C. Cut four pieces of baking parchment, each about 30 cm (12 inches) square. Divide the fennel into piles across each piece of paper.

2 Lay a cod steak on top of each pile and season with black pepper. Squeeze over the lemon juice and scatter with the lemon zest. Lift up the opposite sides of the baking parchment, bring them together at the top and fold over a few times to seal. Fold over the open ends and tuck underneath the fish to make a sealed parcel.

3 Place the parcels on a baking tray and bake for 15 minutes, until just cooked through.

4 Meanwhile make the sauce. Spray a small saucepan with the cooking spray and stir fry the shallots with a couple of tablespoons of water, until softened.

5 Squeeze in the lemon juice and allow to bubble, and then remove from the heat and stir in the lemon zest, dill and fromage frais. Season and serve with the fish.

party time

Encourage your children to have fun with these party ideas that are so much more exciting than crisps and sausage rolls. Everyone will love them, and no one will realise these recipes are wholesome, low in fat and salt.

From **buffets** to **picnics**, **Indian** to **Mexican**, there are some great party suggestions in this chapter. Go with the themes suggested or mix and match as the mood takes you. Just enjoy yourselves.

easy buffet

HOUMOUS WITH ROASTED VEGETABLES
A tasty new way to make and serve houmous.

Serves 8 as party food ■ Takes 30 minutes to prepare, 35 minutes to cook ■ ⓥ

8 large carrots, peeled, cut in half crossways and then into wedges
4 courgettes, cut in half crossways and then into wedges
500 g (1 lb 2 oz) sweet potatoes, peeled and cut into wedges
1 cauliflower, divided into large florets
4 tablespoons balsamic vinegar
low fat cooking spray
2 large red peppers, halved and de-seeded
600 g (1 lb 5 oz) canned chick peas
2 garlic cloves, crushed
juice of a lemon
freshly ground black pepper

1 Preheat the oven to Gas Mark 8/230°C/fan oven 210°C. Place the carrots, courgettes, potatoes and cauliflower on a large roasting tray and sprinkle with the balsamic vinegar and black pepper. Spray with the cooking spray.

2 Lay the pepper halves on top of the other vegetables, skin side up. Roast for 35 minutes, turning the vegetables occasionally with a fish slice to prevent them from sticking to the bottom.
3 Remove the pepper halves after 15–20 minutes, when the skin has blistered and charred. Wrap in a plastic bag and set aside until cool enough to handle. Then peel away the skin and chop roughly. Leave the other vegetables to continue for the remainder of the roasting time. Remove the vegetables from the oven and leave to cool.

4 Drain the chick peas, reserving the liquid and put into a food processor with the peeled peppers, garlic, lemon juice and some black pepper. Add enough of the chick pea liquid to allow you to process the houmous to a smooth purée.
5 Check the seasoning and spoon the houmous into a serving bowl. Place the bowl on a large platter and serve with the roasted vegetables around it for dipping.

LEMON SOLE GOUJONS

These tasty goujons are baked in the oven rather than fried. A polenta coating gives them a lovely golden colour.

Serves 8 as party food ■ Takes 15 minutes to prepare, 15 minutes to cook

low fat cooking spray
500 g (1 lb 2 oz) lemon sole, cut into strips
1 egg white
75 g (2¾ oz) dried polenta
freshly ground black pepper
1 lemon, cut into 8 wedges, to serve

For the sauce
100 g (3½ oz) 0% fat Greek yogurt
50 g (1¾ oz) low fat soft cheese
zest of a lemon
1 tablespoon chopped fresh parsley
2 teaspoons capers, chopped finely

1 Preheat the oven to Gas Mark 6/200°C/fan oven 180°C. Spray two baking trays with the cooking spray.
2 Season the strips of fish with black pepper. In a shallow bowl, whisk the egg white with 2 tablespoons of cold water for just a few seconds until foamy. Sprinkle the polenta onto a large plate.

3 Tip the fish strips into the egg white, tossing them to coat. One at a time, roll each fish strip into the polenta to coat it then lay on a baking tray. When all the strips are coated, transfer to the oven to bake for 12–15 minutes, or until golden and crunchy.

4 Meanwhile, make the lemon tartar sauce by mixing together the yogurt with the soft cheese, lemon zest, parsley and capers.
5 Serve the tartar sauce with the fish goujons, garnished with lemon wedges.

SPICY MINI PORK BURGERS

These meaty little bites make an ideal canapé – delicious as a snack.

Serves 8 as party food ■ Takes 10 minutes to prepare, 25 minutes to cook

low fat cooking spray
500 g (1 lb 2 oz) lean pork mince with
    7% fat or less
2 garlic cloves, crushed
1 red chilli, de-seeded and chopped
    finely
1 teaspoon ground coriander
1 teaspoon ground cumin
1 tablespoon chopped fresh
    coriander or parsley
1 small red onion, chopped finely
1 spring onion, sliced thinly
    lengthwise, to garnish

1 Preheat the oven to Gas Mark 5/190°C/fan oven 170°C. Spray two baking trays with the cooking spray.
2 Mix together the pork, garlic, chilli, coriander. cumin, fresh coriander or parsley and red onion. Use wet hands to form the mixture into 24 little burgers. Arrange on the baking trays. Roast in the oven for 25 minutes.
3 Serve the mini burgers on platters, garnished with the spring onion.

Variation You could also try using turkey mince.

CARIBBEAN SALSA SALAD
A fresh, exciting salad. Great on its own or as an accompaniment.

Serves 8 ■ Takes 20 minutes + chilling
■ ⓥ (omit Worcestershire sauce)

2 x 400 g cans red kidney beans, drained and rinsed
1 cucumber, diced
2 x 300 g cans sweetcorn, drained and rinsed
500 g (1 lb 2 oz) cherry tomatoes, quartered
8 spring onions, chopped
4 red peppers, de-seeded and chopped
a large bunch of coriander, chopped

For the dressing
2 garlic cloves, crushed
zest and juice of 2 limes
2 teaspoons Tabasco sauce
6 tablespoons red wine vinegar
1 teaspoon Worcestershire sauce
1 teaspoon ground cumin
freshly ground black pepper

1 Whisk the dressing ingredients together in a bowl or shake together in an empty jam jar.
2 Mix all the salsa ingredients together and then toss in the dressing. This salad is best left for at least 30 minutes in the fridge for the flavours to infuse, but it can be served immediately.

bombay gala

VEGETABLE BALTI

Great flavours and none of the fat associated with a takeaway equivalent. This curry keeps well in the fridge for a few days or could be made in advance and frozen.

Serves 4 ■ Takes 20 minutes to prepare, 30 minutes to cook

■ 🅨 ■ ❋

low fat cooking spray
2 large onions, sliced finely
4 garlic cloves, crushed
2.5 cm (1 inch) piece of fresh root
   ginger, chopped finely
1 small red chilli, de-seeded and
   chopped (optional)
½ teaspoon cumin seeds, crushed
1 teaspoon coriander seeds, crushed
1 tablespoon garam masala
200 g (7 oz) potatoes, peeled and
   diced
4 carrots, peeled and chopped
1 small cauliflower, chopped into
   florets
400 g can chopped tomatoes
300 ml (½ pint) vegetable stock
200 g (7 oz) green beans, chopped
150 g (5½ oz) low fat natural yogurt
a small bunch of fresh coriander,
   chopped (optional)
freshly ground black pepper

1 Heat a large, non stick frying pan and spray with the cooking spray. Stir fry the onions for 5 minutes and season with black pepper. Add a little water to stop them sticking and help them soften. Mix in the garlic, ginger, chilli, if using, and spices and cook for a further 2 minutes.

2 Add the potatoes, carrots, cauliflower, tomatoes and stock, stir together and bring to the boil. Turn down the heat and then simmer for 20 minutes. Add the beans and simmer a further 5 minutes or until the sauce is thick.

3 Remove the pan from the heat and allow to cool a little before stirring in the yogurt and fresh coriander, if using. Serve.

CHICKEN TIKKA

Chicken Tikka is an ideal barbecue dish. However, if the weather isn't being kind, it can be cooked just as easily under a grill.

Serves 4 ■ Takes 25 minutes + marinating ■ ❄ (cooked chicken only)

600 g (1 lb 5 oz), skinless boneless chicken breasts
275 g (9½ oz) low fat natural yogurt
4 tablespoons Tikka curry powder
1 cm (½ inch) piece of fresh root ginger, grated
2 tablespoons lemon juice
½ teaspoon ground cumin
5 cm (2 inches) cucumber, peeled and diced finely
1½ tablespoons chopped fresh mint

To serve
mixed leaf salad
tomato quarters

1 Score each piece of chicken with a sharp knife, taking care not to cut completely through the meat. Place the chicken in a large, non metallic bowl with half of the yogurt and the curry powder, ginger and lemon juice. Mix well to ensure the meat is thoroughly coated, cover and chill to marinate for 2 hours (or longer).
2 Mix the cumin with the remaining yogurt, the cucumber and mint.

3 Preheat the grill to a medium heat or ensure your barbecue is ready. Remove the chicken from the bowl and shake/brush off any excess marinade, leaving just a light coating. Grill the chicken for 6–7 minutes on each side until cooked through. If you'd like to cut the chicken into small bite size pieces, do this after cooking as smaller pieces tend to fall through the barbecue or grill rack.

4 Serve the chicken hot or cold with the cucumber relish, on a simple salad of mixed leaves and tomato quarters.

Tip If you can't find Tikka curry powder, a medium curry powder is fine.

Variation For a spicy cucumber relish, add a pinch of cayenne pepper. You could use it as a dip for vegetable crudités too.

BANANA AND MANGO YOGURT KULFI

We've renovated this fruity dessert by using a large amount of fresh fruit to give it body, adding yogurt instead of cream and sweetening it with artificial sweetener instead of sugar.

Serves 4 ■ Takes 15 minutes to prepare + freezing ■ Ⓨ

600 g (1 lb 5 oz) mangoes
2 bananas, sliced
100 g (3½ oz) very low fat natural yogurt
artificial sweetener
1 egg white (not necessary if using an ice cream machine)

1 To prepare the mangoes, cut down either side of the long flat stone. Peel and chop the flesh. Chop the flesh from around the stone too.

2 Place the mango flesh in a food processor and whizz until smooth. Add the banana slices to the processor, puréeing until no lumps remain. Finally, mix in the yogurt and sweetener to taste. Make it sweeter than you usually like, since freezing will mask the flavour.

3 If you have an ice cream machine, follow the manufacturer's instructions. Or pour the mixture into a shallow plastic container and freeze for about an hour until partially frozen.

4 After an hour, remove the mixture from the freezer and beat. Freeze for a further hour and then beat. Whisk the egg white until stiff and fold in. (You will not to need to use egg white if using an ice cream machine.) Return to the freezer until solid. Serve Indian-style in long elegant glasses.

Note This recipe contains raw egg white. Do not give to young children.

teamwork

'On a rainy day there's no better way to keep the kids amused than getting them cooking in the kitchen. We started by encouraging Dominic a couple of years ago to help us make healthy flapjacks and fairy cakes. Now that he's nine he likes to make supper dishes too. When it was his birthday we made the Mexican Fiesta (pages 158–163) for all his mates in the football team. He enjoyed making the Potato Wedges with Spicy Salsa almost as much as they all enjoyed eating them – they disappeared in a flash.

Mark Ashwell, dad to Megan and Dominic

mexican fiesta

MEXICAN RICE

Hot and fiery, this dish will put you in the mood for a fiesta.

Serves 4 ■ Takes 35 minutes ■ ⓥ
(if not using Worcestershire sauce)

low fat cooking spray
1 teaspoon cumin seeds
2 red onions, chopped finely
3 garlic cloves, crushed
2 small red chillies, de-seeded and
    chopped finely
300 g (10½ oz) dried brown rice
2 red or orange peppers, de-seeded
    and diced finely
600 ml (1 pint) hot vegetable stock
1 tablespoon Worcestershire sauce
1 tablespoon tomato purée
100 g (3½ oz) frozen peas
250 g (9 oz) cherry tomatoes, halved
a small bunch of coriander, chopped
freshly ground black pepper

1 Heat a large, lidded, non stick saucepan and spray with the cooking spray. Fry the cumin seeds until they start to pop. Add the onions and garlic and a tablespoon of water and stir fry for a few minutes, until golden and softened.

2 Add the chillies, rice, peppers, stock, Worcestershire sauce and tomato purée and stir together. Cover the pan and simmer on a low heat for 20–25 minutes, until the rice is very nearly cooked.

3 Add the peas and cover again for 2 minutes. Add the tomatoes and stir through. Season with pepper and scatter with the fresh coriander before serving.

POTATO WEDGES WITH SPICY SALSA

There are many ready-made salsas available but home-made salsa is better since it has a fresher and tangier taste.

Serves 4 ■ Takes 35 minutes ■ ⓥ

4 x 250 g (9 oz) potatoes, scrubbed
    and each cut into six wedges
2 teaspoons paprika
low fat cooking spray

For the salsa
4 tomatoes, skinned, de-seeded and
    diced finely
½ cucumber, diced finely

6 spring onions, sliced finely
2 fat red chillies, de-seeded and
    sliced finely
2 teaspoons lime juice

1 Preheat the oven to Gas Mark 7/220°C/fan oven 200°C.
2 In a medium bowl, mix together the potato wedges and paprika. Place on a non stick baking tray, spray with the cooking spray and cook in the preheated oven for 30 minutes, turning once.
4 Meanwhile, make the spicy salsa by mixing all the ingredients together.
5 Serve the potato wedges with the salsa on the side.

Tip To skin and de-seed tomatoes, drop them into a bowl of boiling water for 10 seconds and then remove with a slotted spoon. The skins should slip off easily. If not, then pop the tomatoes back into the boiling water for another few seconds. Cut the tomatoes into quarters and remove the seeds.

GOOD IDEAS

Party party

Parties are great for getting active. Traditional party games are fun for younger children and will get them running around. Older children, might like a day out ice skating, roller blading or indoor rock climbing. Find something they want to do and either take a picnic or bring everyone home afterwards for a party feast.

Consistency is the key

Whatever you do, make sure you are consistent. Give everyone in the family the same food and keep providing the same messages about healthy choices. Eventually your children will make healthy choices themselves without being prompted.

CHILLI CON CARNE

Serves 8 ■ Takes 30 minutes to prepare, 1½ hours to cook ■ ❋

low fat cooking spray
2 large onions, chopped finely
4 garlic cloves, crushed
600 g (1 lb 5 oz) extra lean beef
 mince with 7% fat or less
4 red peppers, de-seeded and
 chopped finely
450 g (1 lb) mushrooms, sliced
1 small red chilli, de-seeded and
 chopped finely or 1 teaspoon dried
 chilli flakes
1 kg (2 lb 4 oz) carrots, peeled and
 chopped finely
2 tablespoons dried oregano
1 teaspoon paprika
2 bay leaves
1 tablespoon fennel seeds
1 teaspoon ground cinnamon
2 x 400 g cans chopped tomatoes
2 tablespoons tomato purée
1 tablespoon Worcestershire sauce
2 x 400 g cans red kidney beans,
 drained and rinsed
300 ml (½ pint) vegetable stock
freshly ground black pepper
a small bunch of fresh coriander or
 parsley, chopped, to serve

1 Heat a very large, lidded, non stick saucepan or casserole and spray with the cooking spray. Stir fry the onions and garlic for 5 minutes, or until softened, adding a little water if they start to stick.

2 Add the mince and stir fry, breaking it up with a wooden spoon, for 10 minutes, until it is browned all over. Season with black pepper and add all the other ingredients except the coriander or parsley.

3 Bring to the boil and then simmer gently, covered, for 1½ hours, stirring occasionally. Remove the bay leaves. Serve with the coriander or parsley scattered over the top.

SANTA FE SALAD WITH CHILLI AND LIME DRESSING

Enjoy this tangy southwest American inspired salad on a beautiful summer day.

Serves 8 ■ Takes 25 minutes ■ Ⓨ

6 tablespoons 0% fat Greek yogurt
3 tablespoons fresh coriander, chopped finely
1 spring onion, chopped finely
juice of a lime
2 teaspoons artificial sweetener
½ teaspoon chilli powder
425 g can black beans, rinsed and drained
250 g (9 oz) sweetcorn, canned or frozen
300 g (10½ oz) plum tomatoes
1 red pepper, de-seeded and cut into thin strips
450 g (1 lb) Romaine lettuce, shredded

1 To make the dressing, whisk together the yogurt, coriander, spring onion, lime juice, sweetener, chilli powder and 3 tablespoons of water in a small bowl until smooth. Transfer to a jar or a plastic container with a tight-fitting lid and refrigerate until ready to use.

2 In a large bowl or food storage container, layer the remaining ingredients in the order listed. Cover and refrigerate until needed.

3 To serve, spoon the salad ingredients into a bowl. Shake the dressing and then drizzle over the salad. Toss well to coat.

Tip Storing this salad in layers (instead of tossing it immediately) and keeping the dressing separate, helps to keep the salad fresh. It can be stored up to 4 days in the refrigerator.

AUBERGINE CRISPS

These are a delicious alternative to potato crisps. Serve these scattered with cherry tomato halves, rocket leaves and balsamic vinegar.

Serves 4 ■ Takes 15 minutes ■ Ⓨ

2 large aubergines, sliced in half widthways and then into 5 mm (¼ inch) thin slices on the diagonal to give you long semi-circles
low fat cooking spray
freshly ground black pepper

1 Lay the aubergine slices on the grill pan, spray with the cooking spray and then season liberally with black pepper. Grill until golden and then turn the slices over. Spray and season again and grill for a further 2–4 minutes until dried out and golden. Serve warm.

picnic party

SQUASH AND SPINACH TORTILLA
*This dish is utterly delicious.
Serve with a crisp salad of mixed
leaves and cherry tomatoes with
a sprinkling of balsamic vinegar.
Tortillas are also good cold for
picnics and in lunchboxes.*

Serves 4 ■ Takes 30 minutes ■ Ⓥ

**800 g (1 lb 11 oz) butternut squash,
    peeled, de-seeded and diced finely
6 eggs
150 ml (¼ pint) skimmed milk
1 teaspoon Dijon mustard
low fat cooking spray
150 g (5½ oz) baby spinach leaves
freshly ground black pepper**

1 Bring a large saucepan of water
to the boil and cook the squash
for 10–15 minutes, until tender,
then drain.
2 Meanwhile, in a large bowl, beat
together the eggs, milk, mustard
and some black pepper.
3 Heat a large (20 cm/8 inch)
non stick frying pan and spray
with the cooking spray. Then add
the squash and stir fry for a few
minutes, until it turns golden. Add
the spinach and stir fry for a further
few minutes, until wilted. Tip the
egg mixture into the pan.
4 Stir gently together and then
cook over the lowest heat, without
stirring for 10–12 minutes, or
until the bottom is golden and
the tortilla nearly set. Meanwhile,
preheat the grill.
5 Slide the pan under the
preheated grill for a few minutes,
until the top is golden and puffy
and the egg completely set. Cut
into four wedges and serve.

Tip It is necessary to keep the heat
very low so that the bottom of the
tortilla does not burn before it is
cooked through.

HERRING, APPLE AND DILL SALAD

This healthy, clean-tasting salad is perfect for a light summer meal or picnic, or for a summer buffet dish.

Serves 4 ■ Takes 15 minutes to prepare, 20 minutes to cook

750 g (1 lb 10 oz) new potatoes, scrubbed
1 large red onion, sliced thinly
2 red apples, cored and sliced
4 large pickled gherkins or 1 large dill pickle, sliced thinly
150 g (5½ oz) very low fat natural yogurt
1 tablespoon fresh dill, chopped
4 x 75 g (2¾ oz) soused herring fillets
freshly ground black pepper
4 teaspoons chopped fresh dill, to garnish

1 Bring a pan of water to the boil and cook the potatoes until tender. They will take about 20 minutes. Drain thoroughly and set aside.
2 Put the onion, apples, gherkins or dill pickle, yogurt and chopped dill into a bowl and stir together gently.
3 Break the herring fillets into large chunks and add them to the apple mixture. Fold everything together to mix gently.

4 Toss the hot new potatoes through the herring salad, season then serve, garnished with sprigs of dill.

Tip If you prefer, let the potatoes cool before you stir them through the salad.

TURKEY AND WATERCRESS ROLLS

Attractive little rolls that could be prepared and sliced into three or four pieces to serve as finger food for a picnic.

Serves 4 ■ Takes 30 minutes to prepare, 35 minutes to cook

1 teaspoon cumin seeds
a large bunch of watercress, chopped, reserving some for garnish
150 g (5½ oz) low fat soft cheese with garlic and herbs
finely grated zest and juice of a lemon
4 x 100 g (3½ oz) skinless boneless turkey steaks
low fat cooking spray
300 ml (½ pint) vegetable stock
4 tablespoons virtually fat free fromage frais
freshly ground black pepper

1 Preheat the oven to Gas Mark 4/180°C/fan oven 160°C. Heat a large, non stick pan and dry fry the cumin seeds until they pop.

2 Beat together the cumin and watercress (reserving a little to garnish the dish), soft cheese and lemon zest.

3 Place the turkey steaks between two sheets of baking parchment, clingfilm or foil and beat with a rolling pin to flatten them out. Slice each steak in half to make eight thin strips and season.

4 Place spoonfuls of the cheese mixture on the turkey strips and spread. Roll up each strip and fasten with a cocktail stick.

5 Spray an ovenproof dish with the cooking spray and place the rolls in it. Pour over the stock and lemon juice. Season and bake for 35 minutes, until the meat is tender and cooked through.

6 Lift the rolls onto serving plates and stir the fromage frais into the juices. Pour the sauce over the turkey rolls and serve garnished with fresh watercress.

GOOD IDEAS

Variety show
Most children will eat healthy snacks without any fuss, especially if there are no unhealthy treats available. Offer them a choice, such as a bowl of cereal or a bowl of popcorn and they become even more appealing.

Fun for the family

Most people think of party food as crisps, sausage rolls, cake and ice cream. While there's nothing wrong with occasional treats like these, why not be a bit more creative? Get the kids into the kitchen and mix and match some of the ideas from this chapter and from the rest of the book.

Instead of fizzy drinks, try making smoothies such as Mango and Raspberry Smoothie (page 26) or one of the Three Fruit Smoothies (page 24). You could even set up a smoothie bar – older children will love mixing smoothies to their friend's specifications.

Make Raspberry and Banana Muffins (page 28) instead of high calorie cakes. If your family don't like raspberries, try adding other fresh fruit, such as strawberries, instead.

Try wholesome patties instead of regular burgers. Kids will love the Spicy Lentil Patties (page 36), the Turkey Patties with Chilli Apple Sauce (page 46) and the Chick Pea and Vegetable Patties with Coriander Tomato Salsa (page 130). Add wholemeal pitta breads and salad and let everyone make their own exotic burgers.

Finger food is a party favourite, so get the whole family involved to help make Cajun Style Chicken Drummers (page 49) and Lamb Kebabs with Spicy Sauce (page 56).

acknowledgements

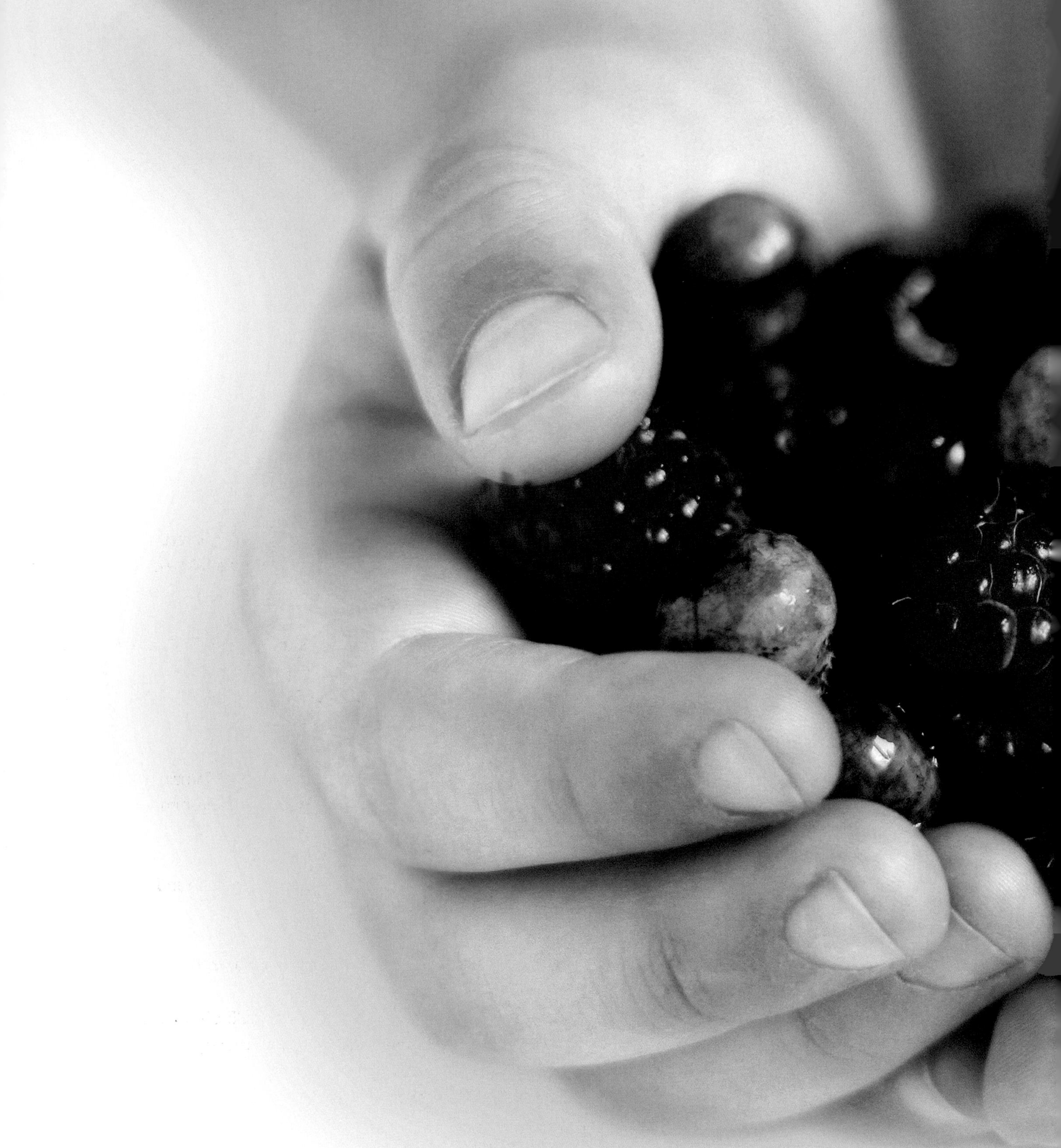

Acknowledgements

A selection of recipes appear courtesy of weightwatchers. co.uk. For more information about Weight Watchers Online visit www.weightwatchers.co.uk

Simon and Schuster and Weight Watchers would like to thank the families featured in this book for their help.
Family photography by Francine Lawrence on pages 55, 107, 134, 156, and Jason Smalley on page 77

Recipes written by: Sue Ashworth, Sue Beveridge, Tamsin Burnett-Hall, Cas Clarke, Roz Denny, Becky Johnson, Kim Morphew and Joy Skipper

Photography by: Iain Bagwell, Steve Baxter, Steve Lee and Juliet Piddington

All other pictures throughout the book from iStockphoto except where indicated below:
Pictures on pages 11, 14, 22, 33, 37, 62, 45, 82, 85, 93, 95, 120, 124 : Getty Images. Picture on page 143: Photolibrary

Design by Meg Georgeson